Relax,

You're Already Perfect

10 Spiritual Lessons... to *Remember*

This book is dedicated to my wife Barbra, whose outer beauty is only surpassed by her Inner Light.

And also to my daughter Erica, who allowed me the experience of unconditional Love.

Acknowledgements

It would take an entire book to personally thank all whose presence in my life shaped the experiences represented here, but I do want to take the opportunity to acknowledge those who made a direct effort to help this book arrive.

Sergey Yevelev, Pat Bell, Pete Masterson, Sandra Tooley, Lea Stuart, Vicki Benson, Linda and Fred Knauer, Dorian Snow, Chris Roerden, David Spivak, Sharice Collins, Ed Bernd, Susan Stone, Gary Kamen, Robin Cohen, Jon Sievert, Doug Ford, Jaime Feldman, Marcos Lederman, Charlie Morecraft, Phyllis Reba, Harry Mesh, Tom Ludlow, Ginger Grancagnolo, Mike Kaplan, Teri Citron, Marcia Platt, Hillary Cige, Chester Yozwick, Carole Parker, Shawn Barone, Angela Gervasi, my brothers Craig and Paul, parents Joyce and Jerry, brother-in-law David, parents-in-law Irving and Judy, and all my clients, seminar participants, friends and relatives whose stories grace these pages.

I would also like to honor the tremendous contributions of three people whose devotion, inspiration, caring, and Love helped make this work possible: Gina Innocente, John Sprung, and David Nemitz.

Contents

Relax, You're Already Perfect

You have done well
and your time has come. Your time is now.
You smiled and you loved smiling;
you hated but did not find Love there;
you shared and loved sharing;
you controlled and destroyed
 and found no Love in doing so;
you created life and truly loved what you created.
You cried, but you never really cried.
You laughed, but you never really laughed.
You lived and died, but only in your mind.
You served the purpose perfectly;
it was always to be that way.
It is now time — to remember.

Relax, You're Already Perfect

The Awakening

During the summer of 1978, an evening of poker with a group of my good friends was neither unusual nor remarkable. However, the events that followed one particular game would change my life forever.

The last hand was dealt a little late, somewhere around two in the morning. I was tired and anxious to get home. To avoid any possibility of slow drivers on the right, I found myself in the left lane of the highway. It turned out there were no other drivers for me to contend with — none sober, that is.

As I headed down the highway, thoughts of the evening entertained my mind. I imagined having a great hand of cards and playing it perfectly, laughing and enjoying the company of my friends. I was always good at using my imagination, and when I reached the top of an overpass and saw two headlights facing me, I remember thinking for a split second that I was imagining that, too.

My next memory is of a conversation about the New York Mets with one of the ambulance personnel. The drunk driver had died instantly. It seems he pulled out of a diner and got on the highway in the wrong direction.

In between states of unconsciousness, I realized I was in the hospital and my parents were holding my hands, crying. They must have been in shock from the sight of the person they saw helplessly lying on the bed before them.

I could barely make out the voices of the doctors who worked above my battered body, as they reported the discouraging prognosis of my condition. They seemed unaware and indifferent to the possibility that I could hear them. I remember thinking, "What's all the fuss?"

For what seemed like an eternity, I remained in critical condition while attempting to suppress unfathomable pain. Regardless of my serious situation, I never doubted I'd pull through.

During my recovery, I enjoyed being referred to as a "living miracle." When people said that it wasn't my time to go, I just nodded, immersing myself within the love and support I was receiving.

I felt special from that time forward, although I now realize that *we are all special; we just don't recognize it.* I also felt less fear than most people and a persistent, growing spiritual sense. It wasn't until much later that I realized the accident had even more of an effect on me than I thought. I had considered myself a scientific, prove-it-to-me kind of person. The non-rational feelings of God and having a spiritual purpose to my life didn't make much sense to my logical mind, but I couldn't get those feelings to leave.

A few years later, I was graduated from college with a degree in jazz studies. I played guitar. I always enjoy telling people that to see the expressions on their faces, as I have traveled in an apparently very different direction from what that degree might lead one to expect. After college, I went into the family automotive parts import/export business because I realized the odds of earning enough money as a musician to pay my bills were poor. I didn't think working in the family business was my ultimate aspiration, but it was convenient. During this period in my life I felt a void, one that I knew would be filled when the time was right. I was drawn to study psychology, biofeedback, various meditative techniques, stress reduction methods, and almost anything else regarding the body-mind-spirit connection. I became a Silva Mind Control lecturer[1] and did extensive research into more supernatural topics such as ESP, near-death experiences, reincarnation, life after death, and other related subject matter.

After years of consideration and reflection, I came to believe that my purpose was to empower others to discover and heal themselves. So I made a commitment to move in the direction of this true calling. Only by assisting others to realize wholeness and happiness have I been able to fill the void I carried with me for many years.

Even after deciding to change professions, I still debated the spiritual nature of my existence. My scientific mind refused to let go com-

---

[1] Silva Mind Control trains people how to access more of their minds.

pletely. For the first time in my life, however, I felt I was on the proper path to uncovering my true purpose. It took a couple of years until I was able to move past my scientific mind-set to understand my true nature and allow myself to feel God completely.

At the time, it was difficult to give up the financial rewards available to me in the family business, but my inner voice was too loud and clear to ignore. It told me that even if I had to make certain sacrifices, I could find my only meaningful success by following my "new" path. I know now that *you never have to give up anything real.*

When I made the decision to change careers, relationships with my friends and family improved, most significantly with my wife.

She was very understanding, and without her support and influence I would not have been able to pursue that change with a clear head. Shortly before, she had battled a painfully debilitating disease. After countless visits to doctors and hospitals, she had almost given up hope she would ever feel relief. A skeptic left with no alternative, she tried a couple of the basic healing techniques I suggested. To her surprise, certain changes in both her physical and psychological nature were immediately apparent.

Her improvement was my final confirmation that I was correct in moving on to that more meaningful direction in my life. How could my logical mind argue with results?

I knew I was still realizing the effects of my accident and would probably continue to for a long time. I didn't know where my journey would lead, but I wasn't worried. I was not alone.

> *"The day of my spiritual awakening was the day I saw —*
> *and I knew I saw — all things in God and God in all*
> *things."*
> — *Mechtild of Magdeburg*

There are many ways people begin to awaken to their spiritual nature: a personal tragedy regarding someone close, a life-threatening illness, the birth of a child, or reaching an age when you just want to know if there is more to life than what you see. Sometimes the awakening — the remembering of who we really are — occurs shortly before physical death. Other awakenings may occur through the encouraging (or nagging) efforts of a loved one or after a long period of questioning and life experience. In my case, the awakening occurred by accident —

literally. It does not matter how we awaken; no method is more significant than another and the result is always the same: once your Spiritual Self begins to awaken, you will never sleep through life again.

About the information in the lessons

This book is about you as the perfect creation of the Universe. This is one of many concepts that you may find difficult to accept as you read. (While the assertion that humankind is intrinsically perfect may strike you as startling, the pages that follow will enable you to discover the truth of this incredibly empowering declaration.)

I derived this information from twenty years of metaphysical research and through "centering," a form of meditation I use to connect and communicate with the Universal Intelligence to acquire or verify information. Only the information that felt right to me in a centered state is included. I knew the words acquired from the centering process were not from my imagination, because I received messages I did not understand at times. These things became clear only after seeing a sign or meditating upon it for clarification. For example, I received information that told me this book should be headed by "lessons" instead of chapters. This didn't make sense, because I believe we already know all truths inherently and have only forgotten them. I programmed for a confirmation sign. The next day I went to my computer and by "chance" ended up in an Internet chat room discussing metaphysics. I had visited such a room only once before. One person wrote, "We need to learn about life's lessons." I answered this with, "I feel we do not need to learn, we already know, we just have to remember." Someone else wrote back: *That is the right answer, we learn how to remember.* I knew it was the answer to my request of the night before. It was a sign for me.

Some of what you read here may seem revolutionary, while other material may be very familiar. Some will seem in line with many known religious beliefs, while other information may seem to challenge the very nature of what you were once told. While I believe that nothing within these pages conflicts with any religion, it may seem to because of a misinterpretation of what was actually meant by the spiritual master that the religion was based on. We are all the same, united with each other and with the Universe. These are my words, your words, God's words.

If you are religious, then as a result of reading this book I believe you will find more meaning in your religion and want to pursue it with new insight and Love.

I'm not telling you to simply accept what I discovered as the truth. What matters is that I do my part to empower you by sharing these discoveries. I believe the energy of these convictions will reach you, because there is only one spiritual truth for all and this cannot be changed.[2] This is my purpose. Do yourself a favor and find out who you are, so you can discover and live your purpose. By doing this you will not only lead a happier, healthier, wiser and wealthier life, but will *consciously* serve that purpose to help make the world a more loving place. This information is presented to help you discover your True Self and the inherent creative abilities you possess. How you proceed from here is entirely up to you.

In filling this book with my experiences, I do not suggest that my insights are *right* and yours aren't. Instead, I offer an alternative (possibly better) way to live. If you're happy, filled with unconditional Love, and consciously following your purpose to make the world a more loving place, it matters not if you live the lessons in this book. If you believe there may be room for more spiritual awareness and increased happiness in your life, then these words may become your words. *I envision a united world surrounded by others who live this same truth, where together we can all experience the wonders of Love without doubt, fear, or worry.*

I use the word "God" throughout the book. If you don't feel comfortable with this word, you may after reading Lesson I, which helps you reassess your concept of God. Throughout the book, I use many variations of the word God, such as: "Higher Power," "Almighty," "One Spirit," "Spiritual Self," "Universal Energy," "Universal Intelligence," "the Universe," or simply "Love." *Don't allow yourself to get too caught up in words.* God created humanity. Humanity created words. The concept of God is actually too great to be described by the limitations of guttural utterances.

---

[2] There are, however, many alternate perspectives and viewpoints to express and help us discover this same truth. We can see this by comparing the core beliefs of the many distinct world religions, finding they are saying the same thing in different ways.

Your beliefs — truths or myths?

The book includes many "myths" about life and God. They are statements I've heard related as "truths" from various sources at one time or another. Most were assertions made by people I have counseled over the years. Their acceptance of these myths blocked or hindered their spiritual development and level of happiness. When clients recognize these beliefs as limiting, they are usually able to break through them and discover greater levels of consciousness. I include these myths exactly as I heard them, so you may more easily recognize what may prevent *you* from remembering who you really are.

This book is written with three objectives:

1) To provide information I received after many years of research and centering. You can *later* decide if any of these pieces fit in your puzzle;

2) To help you to get answers to your questions and receive other types of information and energy directly from the Universe. Sixteen powerful centering techniques, simple and advanced, are provided for this purpose; and

3) To help you apply the information from the lessons, along with the techniques, to many different aspects and situations in your life.

Some of this information will seem as if it is a message *just for you*, just what you wanted, at a time you truly needed it. Who is to say it is not?

Are you sleeping, brother?

"Those who are awake have one world in common. Those who are asleep live each in a separate world."

Heraclitus

According to a popular saying attributed to John Newbern, there are three types of people in the world: those who make things happen, those who watch things happen, and those who say, "What happened?" I think of them as "Thermostats," "Thermometers," and "Sleepers."

The Thermostats

Thermostats control the temperature. They have awakened to their spiritual nature and are consciously and actively enjoying a spiritual experience. If you are in this group, congratulations. You've realized, at least to some degree, that you are much more than a physical body.

A "Thermostat" I know well has said, "I now know I have the ruby slippers on, I just don't know what to do with them." If you are in this group, this book helps you clarify your thoughts and learn some powerful techniques you can apply to every aspect of your life to assist you in your wonderful journey.

The Thermometers

Thermometers report the temperature. They are beginning to awaken to their spiritual essence. They're rubbing their eyes and trying to see what they feel is there, but are too confused and perhaps afraid to focus. If you are in this group, you may be ready to stop going through the motions or letting outside forces control your life.

Some of the questions that "Thermometers" have asked me again and again are:

"What is the purpose to my life?"

"Is there a way to talk with the Universal Intelligence?"

"How do I know what to ask and how to ask these questions?"

"How can I know if the answers I receive are right, and where they came from?"

"In what form would these answers be?"

"How could this information benefit me?"

"Who am I, and why am I?"

If you've asked questions such as these (and you are not already a Thermostat), then you are part of this group. After reading the book and mastering the techniques, you'll have all these questions answered, be able to start making changes in your life, and (for perhaps the first time) see things as they really are. You will become a Thermostat.

The Sleepers

Sleepers are not consciously aware of the temperature around them. If you're in this group, relax and enjoy your sleep. You have all the time in the Universe, and we'll be here to help when you are ready to awaken. If you are reading this book, however, you are probably not a Sleeper. There are no coincidences.

We have arrived at the dawn of a new millennium. If you still aren't certain of what your life is all about or who you really are, the good news is that this book will help you find out. (And more good news — there is no bad news!) It will tell you how to find your purpose, how to know your truth, and how to live it. Sound good? It is!

Are you ready?

There's a great prize available to all of us that few actually achieve in a lifetime. The best part about this delightful contest is that it does not involve luck. Everyone who has the right information about how to play can win! The challenge is to consciously live your life's purpose and to reach enlightenment. The prize is total awareness, happiness, and Love.

It is now time to learn how to remember your true nature and to connect with the Universe. This is a very personal connection.

It is now time to witness perfection!

Lesson I

The Universe is perfect

"I want to know God's thoughts... the rest are details."
— *Albert Einstein*

What would you do if you were the Creator of the Universe? Would you end world hunger? Prevent disease? Bring about world peace? Why doesn't God do these things? There are two reasons: First, God doesn't have to — the spiritual idea of perfection is much different than the human idea of perfection; and second, whether we realize it or not, God conceived us as the perfect creation; it is now *our* responsibility and within our power to create any world experience we desire. We can do that right now.

This lesson may challenge your concept of God, but it will also shed light on the apparent chaos in the world. Its intention is to help you create a happier life for yourself by seeing things from a new perspective.

Why should you listen to me? After all, I know nothing about the nature of your life. But there are a lot of things I've experienced about the nature of my life, and I believe that these inner feelings are spiritual truths that can be felt by everyone. We all have the ability to consciously connect to the Universal Spiritual Energy from within. This enables us to know the truth by feeling it, instead of using only logic or other mental faculties. You too can know the truth. In fact, you already do, *remember?*

About fifteen years ago, I began to meditate regularly to improve my athletic ability. I had read a book about the power of the mind in sports and wanted to improve as a semi-pro softball player. I practiced constantly, lifted weights, studied films of the best players, and, sure enough, I improved. But it wasn't until I began to connect with a remarkable energy force that things really changed. I centered myself within the power of this energy two or three times a day, and, not only did I achieve all my goals in softball, but I got a bonus. I discovered something wonderful. I realized that the energy force I was connecting with was God.

At first I didn't know it was God, but I came to recognize the Almighty after a while. And this wonderful presence spoke with me. I'd ask questions and get answers. No, I didn't hear voices, but I did get some incredible feelings and signs that brought results when acted on. I know many might question that it was God with whom I communicated, but this truth (and presence) is so strong that each person can feel and know it if they allow themselves. Nineteenth-century Bible interpreter Thomas Troward said that truth will "appeal to our feelings and our reason with a power that carries conviction with it."

Connecting with the Universal Energy helped me achieve my desired sports goals. After a while, I decided that if this powerful connection worked so well for sports, why not try to improve the other aspects of my life as well. This was all part of my spiritual journey — a journey that has taken me places I've never even dreamed of going. It's a journey that more and more of us are realizing we are on. Being conscious of this journey has created a life of abundance for many people, complete with happiness, health, wisdom, and wealth. *It can do the same for you!* All you need to remember is that the Universe is perfect, and… the rest will be details.

The perfection of the Universe

"The immanence of God gives reason for the belief that pure chaos is intrinsically impossible."
Alfred North Whitehead

When you were young you were probably told that God was perfect. Most likely, you didn't stop to think seriously about what embracing this concept would mean to your life. If you do now, and you understand and live this as the truth, you will never look at your life (or the world) in the same way again.

Instead of trying to prove that spiritual perfection exists, accept, for a moment, that it does, and things may start to become clear.

In the movie *Crimes and Misdemeanors*, an elderly man decided that he would live his life "as if" God existed and there was perfection in the Universe. He remarked, "[I] will have lived a better life for having believed and acted as if [this were true]." This is exactly what I ask you to consider doing now. If God does not exist, then it won't matter anyway. If the Almighty is not perfect, than what chance do you have? Why not begin to live your life in the ideal? I propose that by living this philosophy you will enjoy your life more. I also propose that you *will* definitely know that this is the truth when you are ready to experience it.

Let us now look at the world through perfect eyes.

The perfect process of the Universe

Everything you see, feel, hear, taste and touch is part of a perfect evolutionary process of "re-discovery"[1] created by the Universal Intelligence and recreated by us every moment. God is all. God is whole. God is Love and all things in their purest forms. But Love cannot exist alone. According the renowned psychiatrist Carl Jung, "Wholeness is possible only via the coexistence of opposites. In order to know the light, we must experience the dark." In order for Love to be known, the Universe creates the experience of "what Love is not." By knowing what Love is not, we remember, appreciate, and live in the truth of Love. This is the perfect process of re-discovery.

We, in the physical dimension, experience not only joy and peace, but also anger, grief, and all other painful experiences available to humanity. Everything is created so we may know the highest, purest form of ourselves, which is complete Love. Understanding this process may be the most empowering inspiration of your life.

Ever hear the joke, "Why did the man keep hitting his hand with the hammer?" The answer is, "Because it felt so good when he stopped." Sure, this is pretty funny, but it's actually a very good example of the perfect process. We need "bad" experiences to be able to move us closer

---

[1] We do not first "discover" Love, as Love is all there ever was.

to the truth — to remember we are part of God and to know that there is nothing that is actually bad. We should be thankful for all experiences, for without them, there would be no chance to obtain the ultimate objective: the re-discovery of Love for the One Spirit, of which we are all a part.

You may think, "Pain doesn't sound 'perfect' to me." Understand that we are physical beings and our idea of perfection is a concept we create. Spiritual perfection of the Universe is beyond physical definition, but it may help to clarify things a bit. Did you know that a perfect, beautiful, white light is actually made up of *all* the colors in the spectrum? Without these other colors there would be no white light. Does knowing this about the nature of pure white light make it any less perfect and beautiful? Spiritual enlightenment includes a change of how one views the world. To be more enlightened, look to the light!

Any perception that is subject to change is not God's perfection but a judgment created by the human mind. For example, some people would say a perfect diamond is one without any flaws and bluish in color. Others, however, might prefer a colorless diamond instead of one that's blue. If even one person perceives a flaw due to the diamond's color, it can not be universally perfect. The perfection of the Universe is the only true perfection, because it is universal and will sustain itself throughout eternity.

At one time Europeans and Americans considered a plump body as perfect. Now the perfect body is considered by most to be thinner. Some people, in an attempt to be more "perfect," actually harm themselves by trying to conform to this judgment.[2] No harm can come from the spiritual perfection of the Universe. It *never* changes; never has and never will. When you *experience* this truth, (1) you will know it to be true perfection, (2) you will realize that the physical world is a perceptual illusion, (3) you will discover the key to ultimate peace and happiness, and (4) your life will never be the same.

Experiencing life's seemingly flawed occurrences is how the Universe re-discovers, by comparison, the only real perfection and reality

---

[2] As in the examples of anorexia and bulimia.

[3] The master carpet weavers of India would intentionally create one small flaw in their rugs so that perfection remained God's handiwork. But it also showed their awareness of the perfect process by understanding and allowing this small contrast.

— true, pure Love.[3] We re-discover the light after we experience darkness. We re-discover the absence of pain when we stop hitting our hands
with hammers. And we re-discover Love after we experience what Love
is not.

Michaelangelo seemed to utilize the perfect process of re-discovery
when he created the statue of David. He began with a block of stone
and chipped away everything he believed was *not* David. We will use
the same process as we chip away at the many limiting beliefs and painful illusions we initially see — to reveal the beauty that remains.

Let us begin to reveal the beautiful perfection of the Universe by
first disposing of what God is not. We do this by looking at some of the
limiting beliefs that cause people to lose faith in the Almighty (and
themselves). These restricting conceptual ideas are usually created by
fear.

Myth: "There is no God."

The client who expressed this to me was depressed. I expect that if
she truly believed this myth, she would not have sought out my services
as a spiritual therapist. As our initial session unfolded, it became apparent that her current life situation had simply caused her to lose faith in
the Almighty. But some people really don't believe in God. This is perfectly fine, and they will still serve the universal purpose for their creation by experiencing the physical world: *re-discovering Love for the
Universe and re-membering who they are in the "process."* I've heard people
say, "I don't *need* to believe in God," but this philosophy severely limits
their potential for happiness. True happiness can only be attained by
awakening to a complete understanding and unity of body, mind, and
spirit. You may disagree and think, "but I'm happy now." The happiness
you may feel now is an illusion if it can disappear as the events surrounding your life change. True happiness comes from within, is permanent, and includes a unity of body, mind and spirit.

The only way people who don't believe in God, or how powerful
God's creations are, will realize the incredible potential awaiting them
is to experience the Universal Energy for themselves. (This applies
equally to people who do believe in God conceptually but are not inti-
mately connected to the Divine.) Only then can they answer their own
questions about the *benefits* of believing. Experiencing leads to knowing, and knowing reveals more experiences.

Application: Believing is seeing

Use the Basic Centering Technique (at the end of this lesson) and think about God. Do not try to force anything to happen, but instead relax and repeat the phrase, "God is perfect, the Universe is perfect, everything makes sense," over and over, and wait to feel something more peaceful than you felt before. Try to feel the presence of God *within* you. This feeling will be one of calm and fearlessness, with a sense of knowing that everything is where it should be for you and everyone else. With practice, you will be able to experience this more easily and will not forget the feeling.

Once you feel this powerful presence, begin to study the world around you. Marvel at the sky or a tall building. Listen to the wind as it whistles through the trees. Remove your shoes and feel the earth beneath your feet. Savor the taste of an apple. Go to the beach and breathe in the intoxicating redolence of an ocean breeze. Allow yourself to recognize the perfection of God in all these things. You'll feel the same sensation of peace and fearlessness as you will when connected to your Higher Self in a centered state.

Can God be measured?

If you doubt God's existence and perfection, you don't know what you're missing! Once you suspend or remove your disbelief, you can unlock the power of the Universe and use it to your benefit and that of all humanity. I have witnessed the results of such power time and again: wonderful relationships, financial wealth, and the remarkable ability to heal oneself and others. You can have anything truly desirable, do anything you really want, be who you really want to be, and most importantly, live a life of undiminished Love and happiness. Remember the old adage, "Try it, you'll like it!"

There are many reasons why people do not have faith in God — disappointment, physical and emotional abuse, tragedy, you name it. When listening to some of these painful stories it is understandable why people choose to "disown" or give up on God. This leads us to another myth.

Myth: "God is a supreme being."

For people with no faith in God, it is helpful to realize that it's most likely not God but their *concept* of what the Almighty is that they don't have faith in. If you think of God as a *being,* maybe even a person who looks just like you, then you've underestimated the Universal Energy and created God in *your* image, instead of the other way around. It is limiting to conceive of the Universal Energy as only a being. God is everywhere, in everything and everyone. If you've had a very painful life experience — or believe you haven't felt or witnessed any miracles in your life — it's easy to see why you may feel disappointed, discouraged, or apathetic. Perhaps you were once told that God is perfect and your intelligent mind assumed that, if it were true, neither you nor anyone else would have to suffer. This is a misconception of the perfect process God created, and quite possibly the reason for your disbelief.

If you don't believe, or lack faith in God, there is still some very good news for you. If you are interested in taking advantage of the tremendous energy and personal growth available to you by accepting the Almighty as part of your belief system, the words that follow are for you. *God is within you, waiting to be remembered and expressed.*

In my work with clients who had lost faith (or didn't believe) in God, I found them able to accept the alternate concept described below. As a result of this "new" idea, these people were able to develop a personal connection with the Universal Energy and were reportedly much happier for it. Use this alternative concept of God if it is more helpful, or if your concept is not working *for* you, so you can more easily benefit from the magnificent power of the Universe.

Even if you do not like scientific jargon, bear with me on this. There may be something very interesting in it for you.

There is energy all around us. It is magnetic and electrical, and it is constantly vibrating at many different frequencies. This "electro-magnetic field" can be measured with scientific instruments. One strong frequency, when measured, reads about ten cycles per second.[4] Therefore, the energy that surrounds every single molecule in the Universe could be measured at a strong frequency of around ten cycles per second.

The human brain is also made up of vibrating energy. Where the heart is measured in beats per minute, the brain is measured in cycles per second — brain waves, and there are many different levels of these vibrations.

---

[4] Cycles per second is also referred to as hertz (Hz).

Currently, you are probably in the Beta (or "wakeful") state, producing frequencies more in the range of fourteen to twenty-one cycles per second. People usually use one side of the brain more than the other during conscious states. In Beta, you predominantly use the left part of your brain for logic and analytical purposes.

There are other ranges as well. Delta is one of the slowest frequencies, fluctuating between two to four cycles per second. Delta is predominant when we are babies, until we learn to develop higher brain waves, and when we near physical death. Little is known about the function of Delta.

Theta waves are a bit faster than Delta, or around four to seven cycles per second. Theta is prevalent during deep sleep and is associated with very little conscious activity. Theta brain waves are observable when we elicit the "fight or flight" defense system, inherent in all creatures, when the body reacts to protect itself from a real or perceived threat.

For humankind, the strongest frequencies occur in the Alpha range, typically between seven and fourteen cycles per second. This was the first, and most powerful frequency, discovered by science — hence, the name Alpha, from the first letter of the Greek alphabet. In an Alpha state we use the right (for creativity) and the left (for logic) sides more equally. Most musicians and artists emit high levels of Alpha waves while expressing their talents. Alpha can be easily measured during our dream state when the creative dimension comes alive.

Now comes the fun part! Somewhere in the middle of the Alpha range is the strongest receptive state we can experience. It is where we unlock our true potential — where we are "centered." The strongest part of the Alpha range is around ten cycles per second, the same powerful energy as in the Universe! When you center yourself at this frequency, you are more connected with, and more able to tap into, the power of everything around you. Think of how you tune in a radio station. If you are a little off, you hear the station's broadcast, but not as clearly as when you center the dial in its frequency. If you want to listen to the beautiful music of God: tune in!

If you've had difficulty with your concept of God as a being, consider this centered energy to be God if you wish. (You can, of course, call this energy the "Higher Intelligence" or any other name you choose.) For you, God could be the Universal Energy that surrounds and is in all things — a source that you can link with by learning how to "center" yourself. If you've lost faith in God by believing the Almighty to be a person, this alternative concept should help rid you of this limiting notion.

With this in mind, even agnostics and atheists can find it possible to have a connection with God (or, the Universal Energy). Through this connection, anyone can tap into the energy that surrounds them to create a happier life for themselves, their loved ones, and the rest of humanity.

How the Universe works

You may still find it difficult to understand how some things could be part of the perfection of the Universe. Most likely, you'll need some time in connection with the Universal Energy to feel the truth. If, however, you believe the Universe to be perfect at the outset, you'll have an easier time seeing how apparent chaos is part of the perfect process.

Let's now reveal how God works. Once you are able to feel this, you'll know the true meaning of perfection.

Myth: "God decides what's right and wrong."

One of the most confusing aspects of religion to me, and to many others taught in the same way, is that we must do what is *right* by God — or else. I never understood this. It just didn't feel comfortable to me. To this day I consider myself a spiritual person, but not a religious one in the traditional sense. Most likely in my youth, I missed the message in my religion by taking it literally.[5] I suspect many of you did as well.

As far as "right" or "wrong" goes, I always felt it was subjective, so I also found it hard to accept the concept of right and wrong using anyone else's parameters, including legal criteria. Most laws are necessary and beneficial as guidelines: that is, as a generally accepted course of "preferred" behavior. But laws do not necessarily tell us what is right.

Is it wrong to speed?

Is it wrong to speed to the hospital?

Is it wrong to steal food to feed your children?

There are no simple answers to these questions. *From a spiritual per-*

---

[5] Philosopher and Bible interpreter Emmet Fox states, "the words [in the Bible] cover a far wider meaning than we attach to them."

spective, there is no right or wrong. Everything we are is perfect, whether we realize it or not, because we are perfect creations of the Universe. (You may not yet believe humanity is a perfect creation. Lesson II reveals this extraordinary truth).

Only we, preferably in a centered state,[6] can decide what is right and wrong for us. These choices help define who we are. God will not decide anything for us. The Universe created a perfect process of rediscovery and this process needs no further deliberation. Consider this: if our souls were eternal, living hundreds of lives, and each incarnation brought us closer to experiencing our True Self and helped the Universe re-discover Love, why would anything we do in any one life concern the Higher Intelligence? Each life would be just a drop of water in an ocean of eternity. We would all end up in the same place regardless of any one life experience. As we are eternal beings (Lesson VII), this speculation is actually the truth and part of God's perfection.

Myth: "God sits in judgment of me."

One of the most difficult concepts to grasp is that God is non-judgmental, even though this is the only way a perfect God could be. Because there is no right or wrong from a spiritual perspective, God doesn't need to be judgmental. For us to be judged by God, we would have to be good or bad. Sometimes, the things we do are good or bad, but not to God — only to ourselves in the physical world. We will discuss this further in the next lesson.

God would not judge God's own creation. Perfection can only create perfection. The Universe, being perfect, only observes and experiences this perfection. An assumption that the Almighty would not create perfection is to challenge God's ability, which eventually leads to doubt and fear.

Some people use fear tactics to try to convince others to believe a certain way. Unfortunately, some civil "authorities" and organized religions do this. It is quite sad to use fear to control others. Clergy who tell their congregations that they must act a certain way to be accepted by God, and then claim that God is non-judgmental are contradicting them-

---

6 Making choices in a centered state allows us to choose with Love instead of choosing out of fear, or any other of the emotional distractions of the physical world.

selves. Do you think a non-judgmental God would prefer one human over another? One religion over another? Would this be unconditional Love? This brings us to the next myth.

Myth: "God chooses (blesses) one over another."

The winning prizefighter thanks the Lord for choosing him over his opponent. The rich thank God for being "truly" blessed. The poor curse God for not "choosing" them to be rich. Each army says, "God is on our side." This is ridiculous. The essence of the Universe is non-judgmental and unconditionally loving. To assume that God would love or choose any person or people over another would be to challenge God's perfection. It would make God human.[7]

We were all created in the image and likeness of God. There is no right or wrong in God's eyes: there is no good and bad. These are labels that we choose for ourselves and others. If I were to decide that something such as poverty is bad, then poverty is bad for me. Those who take a vow of poverty believe it is a holy act. Good and bad are choices only we ourselves can make.

Truth: God did not create victims

> "Nonviolence is born of the shared experience of the pain of violence."
>
> Matthew Fox

The hardest thing for many people to come to terms with is the concept of a perfect God who would allow the many seemingly horrible experiences that we go through. Our logical minds simply cannot conceive of some situations as beneficial in any way. When, in a centered state, I posed this question to the Spiritual Intelligence, I felt the answer instantly and knew it was right. (How this is accomplished will be explained in Lesson III, so please "stay tuned.") A purpose can be found in all things that happen, and all events eventually lead us to know Love. We don't understand some situations as they happen, and others we may not understand in this lifetime. But everything that happens is

---

[7] This is not to suggest that we are not perfect. Only that God does not possess our illusory human limitations.

part of the perfect process and is directed at helping humanity as a whole. Life doesn't start and it doesn't end, and this process allows us to experience all we can in this human form.

In God's perfection there is no spiritual suffering, only opportunities to experience pain so we may eventually know pleasure and Love by comparison. Mohammed saw this truth, Moses experienced it, Jesus demonstrated it, and Buddha lived it. We can know this truth as well.

As I laid in pain and agony after that 1978 car accident, I could have easily fallen into the "why me" trap and become quite depressed. With a depressed and negative attitude, I may not have pulled through. Instead, in my heart I felt that there was a reason I experienced this trauma. I didn't know what that reason was, but I was sure it would become clear to me one day. I was in pain, but I didn't feel like a victim. This book is a product of that experience.

Truth: Everything that happens has purpose

An example that explains the mystery of God's perfection can be seen in Christopher Reeve, a talented and versatile actor who entertained millions of people on the big screen. Best remembered, perhaps, for his portrayal of Superman, he seemed to have everything until a horse-riding accident caused complete quadriplegic paralysis. How could this be perfection? Certainly the hands of fate did not seem to be in Mr. Reeve's favor. Seeing the apparent tragedy in what happened is the usual human way to judge events. It is not, however, the spiritual reality.

Mr. Reeve is now an American hero who's touching more lives in so many very special ways than ever before. He provides hope, Love, and inspiration to everyone by making the world a more loving place through his "sacrifice." Now, he truly is a "superman." This is the perfect process.

When a soul allows its physical self to be "sacrificed," born with physical challenges, or become disabled in one way or another, it is because this soul has chosen to move the world in a special way before it took up residence in its current human form. A soul who allows us to re-discover Love in this manner, does so to fulfil its specific purpose for this lifetime.[8]

---

[8] Helen Keller was another beautiful, inspirational figure who demonstrated this process.

There is no actual sacrifice in the spiritual reality, as we are all eternally connected to all other souls and to the Divine Spirit. What looks like an individual sacrifice is actually part of the perfect process of our spiritual development as a whole. You may have heard of the expression, "sacrificing a thumb to save the hand." Think of the Christopher Reeve example as (temporarily) sacrificing a thumb to *enlighten* the hand.

People may not even be aware of the purpose they chose for this life. It is imperative that we forget why we came to this dimension if we are to experience what we believe is reality (you will understand why in Lesson II). Mr. Reeve did not have to experience that particular injury or accident either. It didn't matter how it happened. His soul made a decision to help humanity in a powerful way before Mr. Reeve was born, and the free will of his mind created and effected his purpose for him when the time was most propitious.

This is the same with all apparent suffering. Although it is a most difficult idea to grasp, especially when we see innocent people (particularly children) facing unbelievable physical and mental horrors, it is important to not lose sight and to understand the perfect process of rediscovery created by the Universal Intelligence. There is no other way. Our choice is to either see the purpose in these situations or dwell in the misery of an apparently chaotic world. Which way would make sense from an eternal spiritual perspective? Which way feels more like Love?

Truth: God has no preferences

We are all equal in God's eyes. Those eyes see no religion better than another, nor does it matter if you even belong to one. There is no job better than another. There is no race, creed, or belief better than any other. Nothing about your life experience is preferred by God. Eventually, you will experience everything. In a spiritual sense, time and space do not even exist. This means that it does not matter to God *when* anything happens or does not happen, because everything is happening at the same time.[9] Allow yourself to relax, think, and feel the truth, and you will see that everything is eternal and wonderful.

Application: Developing a God trigger

Try to develop a trigger to help you relax and think about God. A

---

[9] The illusion of time is discussed further in Lesson IV.

trigger is something that reminds (or "triggers") you to remember to think or do something. For you, it may be something like a red traffic light. Every time you stop at a red light, for example, remind yourself to take a deep breath and repeat mentally, "My eyes are open, God is within me, I need never be afraid again." The more you remember to think about God, the more likely you are to achieve greater happiness from being in that mind-set.

A trigger can also remind you to take a deep diaphragmatic breath from time to time, especially when you feel stress. Just being able to relax is the first step to knowing who you truly are.

Myth: "God rewards and punishes."

Clients who have repeated statements like this to me always felt they were being punished by God, which made them powerless to overcome their problems. If you can challenge the myths you have read so far, then you may understand that the Almighty would neither punish nor reward any human being because there is nothing we do that is good or bad in God's eyes. The Universal Intelligence gave us the opportunity to experience the human existence as part of our quest to uncover the true nature and beauty of Love. We reward and punish ourselves through our free will.

It doesn't matter to God whether you go to a church, mosque, ashram, or synagogue. You will not be rewarded by God if you go, nor punished if you do not. The Almighty does not reward the boxer for praying before he tries to beat up his opponent in the ring. You will not lose any fight because you do not pray. You will enter the kingdom of heaven no matter what you do, and eventually realize heaven is already within us all. Always has been, always will be.

The word "blasphemy" is a concept that humankind created to describe disrespect to God. It doesn't exist in the spiritual reality. Our Higher Power is within us. It *is* us, and there's nothing we can do to change that. If anything, blasphemy is believing the Universe to be anything less than perfection. Even this does not matter to the Almighty. It does matter to us, affecting how we live, how we choose to experience this lifetime, and how happy we can be.

Myth: "God wants us to be …"

If you *want* something that suggests you are without it. Perfection lacks nothing. If you have enough money to live as you desire, you don't need more. If you have enough security, you are not insecure. If you have enough Love within you, you do not need to get more from the outside. This does not suggest that we can't experience and enjoy more Love by sharing it, only that we do not need to get it from an outside source. God has created us perfectly within ourselves. Uncover that perfection by remembering who you are!

God is not needy. God has everything already (and so do we). Because God needs nothing from us except to just "be," the Universe operates perfectly, with unconditional Love and without the need for us to do what we think we must or should be doing. The pressures of life are created in our individual minds, not the Universal Mind.[10] You do not have to fear God, or anything for that matter. Just stay awake and live happily!

The Universal Intelligence did not set up any tests for humanity. It is not God's design that anyone wins or fails. The Almighty experiences the physical world with and through us. We can just enjoy the ride, marvel at the incredible wonders in and around our lives, and create our own situations for the One Spirit to experience.

Application: See a purposeful world

Take a trip somewhere you've never been and try to see God in something new. Remind yourself that God is looking back at you, and that it is all purposeful and perfect.

Watch a sunrise and lovingly feel the power of the Universe — this is your power, too.

Spend time observing the perfect creation of nature. Feel how everything is the way it should be. While in the presence of nature, enter a centered state using the Basic Centering Technique (on page 41) and repeat the following affirmation until you feel it as truth: "I have faith in the power of God and know that the perfect process of re-discovery is always occurring for my benefit and the benefit of my brothers and sisters."

Myth: "God is to be worshipped."

The client who told me this myth didn't look at the word "worship"

---

[10] The difference between the Universal and individual minds, as well as the soul and spirit, is explained in Lesson IV.

in a healthy way for her. Yes, look at God in awe, but only as you look at yourself and every other being in the same way. If you idolize a statue more than your own self, you diminish your own perfection and that of God who created you.

We are all equal in God's eyes. Different, perhaps, but none better, none worse. God also created the person represented in the statue as equal to you. In an awakened world, each of us would remember that he or she is completely wonderful and worthy of the respect that we would give to a Jesus, a Moses, a Krishna, or a Buddha. Only when we re-discover who we really are do we free ourselves from the fear and worry that keeps us feeling smaller than others.

Never doubt God's power or your own. The Almighty is in us all. In Moses, Buddha, Jesus, Gandhi, Mike, Sally, and Fran. Wouldn't it be wonderful if we actually listened to the great spiritual leaders who gave us the message that we can do anything they can? They knew we were all equal. They knew we were as good as they. Only we, with our self-doubt and fear, find it hard to believe we could possibly be as wonderful as God or God's teachers.

Some people who are spiritually asleep seem to have a need to idolize someone or something outside themselves. They need to create an image of an entity bigger than them. They do this hoping that someone will someday save them from their fears, which relinquishes the responsibility for doing this for themselves. They already have the power to do this, and just like Dorothy in the *Wizard of Oz,* forgot that this power is within them. They choose to create a personal perspective of inferiority and subservience instead of a reality of equality and perfection.

This is not God's intention. We were given everything that was given to the great leaders. They just opened their eyes and hearts and knew. You can do the same. *Never* tell yourself that you are anything less than incredible, anything less than anyone else,[11] and anything less than God. We were created in God's image: nothing more and nothing less. Fear makes us feel we must worship someone outside ourselves. Fear is something we create to let us know when we fear no longer and know Love by comparison. There is nothing real to fear, ever. In the spiritual reality, fear doesn't even exist.

---

[11] This does not mean that everyone has the same physical, intellectual, or artistic abilities, but these abilities vary in the physical dimension only. There is perfection in our spirit, and our spirit is One.

Myth: "We need to be saved."

Being saved is a religious concept, and it may be helpful at this time to mention something about the interpretation of the masters' messages. You may think some of these myths are truths taught in the Judeo-Christian tradition, and by calling them myths, I'm contradicting the Bible[12] (or other religious books).

Let's take one quote from the Bible and see how there can be interesting alternate meanings to the same words: Jesus said, "Except ye believe that I AM, ye shall die in your sins." When I ask people what their interpretation of this quote is, almost invariably they think it means that anyone who doesn't follow the word of God will be punished.

The obvious (more literal) interpretation is not necessarily the only one and, more than likely, the literal answer is misleading. The Bible was written in a manner to make you think for yourself, not to give obvious answers. What could an alternative meaning to these words be? What meaning could be found that would confirm the absence of sins in God's eyes (or even the reality of death, for that matter)?

First, understand that the words "I AM" are synonymous with God.[13] Remember also that the Bible says "The Kingdom of Heaven is within."[14] The interpretation I received while centered was this: if you don't believe that God exists within you and that you are incapable of sinning in God's eyes, then you will *believe* death is real (at the time your physical self is dying) and die *believing* that you have sinned because you didn't discover the truth during your life. You will die unhappily with that belief in mind only to later realize you suffered needlessly.

Notice also that the words say in *your* sins, not sins of God. This passage from the Bible is tremendously empowering. It says you needn't dwell in fear and guilt, and that it is within your power to choose what you believe and, therefore, how you live.

By her own words, the client who expressed this myth to me had already lived with too much guilt her entire life stemming from her belief that she was a bad child and now living in sin.

---

12 Emmet Fox points out that the "Plan of salvation," which is heard in many religious sermons, is not found anywhere in the Bible or the Koran.

13 When Moses was on the mountain and asked what the name of God was, he was told, "I AM that I AM." (Exodus 3:6, 14.) God simply is.

14 Luke 17:21

To suggest that God's creation needs to be "saved" is to suggest that God created something less than whole. However, if you instead say you would love to remember who you are and *save yourself from the illusions of fear and suffering, you are on the right track. You don't need to do anything to save your soul, but if you're not awake you're not consciously aware of the unbelievable spiritual experiences each of us can have in this physical state.* If this is the case, more than likely you will be unhappy. There is nothing wrong if you sleep through this lifetime, and you will not burn in "hell" no matter what you do. Either now or later you will experience all life has to offer before progressing spiritually to an understanding that transcends the physical illusion — an understanding that allows you to be happy and free.

Lesson I summary:

The Universe is perfect. By accepting and living this as truth, you come to understand the world and realize why things happen. This will allow you to experience true freedom. Not accepting this keeps you fearful, preventing you from becoming spiritually enlightened. More important, it keeps you from reaching your potential for Love and happiness in this lifetime. Remember, the existence of painful or unpleasant things in the world does not undermine the perfect process of the Universe; it complements it. Believe first, and then you'll see and know the perfection of the Universe.

Are you ready to accept the possibility of spiritual perfection in the Universe? If so, open your heart, and your mind will follow.

Here are the first of sixteen powerful centering techniques described in this book. If you feel uncomfortable during any of the techniques, stop and try again at another time. If you continue to have difficulty with them, get assistance from someone experienced to guide you. Practice all the techniques in a sitting position so that you do not fall asleep (unless that is what you are trying to do).

Technique # 1

The Perfect Breath

Purpose:

A partial list of benefits to practicing the Perfect Breath Technique on a regular basis includes enhanced ability to effectively produce visualization and mental imagery; better oxygen circulation; improved digestion; increased energy; general relaxation; improved sleep; decreased physical and emotional pain; reduced fear and anger; a reduced effort of the heart; lengthening of life; and a pathway to feeling and using the Universal Energy.

Application:

The Perfect Breath Technique is used to start the Basic Centering Technique (on page 41) and whenever and wherever you need to relax.

Procedure:

Breathe deeply and slowly, preferably through your nose, from the diaphragm, (just above the stomach), trying to expand this area first as you inhale. You may want to imagine filling your stomach with air as if you were blowing up a balloon. After your diaphragm is full, begin filling your chest with a smooth rolling motion, remembering not to release the air in your diaphragm as your lungs fill. If it helps, place one hand on your stomach and the other on your chest while you breathe. As you breathe in, your bottom hand should rise. When you fill your lungs by "rolling" more air into your chest, your other hand will rise as well. Fill both your diaphragm and your lungs before exhaling through your mouth.

How it works:

Breathing deeply from the diaphragm first, allows you to take in much more air than breathing through the chest only. This allows you to relax more deeply than a breath into the lungs alone can. Extra air helps you remove stress and "bad" air while life-giving oxygen cleanses your entire body. Concentrating on breathing also helps block out distractions around you.

Additional comments:

Whenever you think of it, take a *Perfect Breath* during the day. It is one of the healthiest things you can do for yourself. Program some triggers, such as a ringing phone, to remind you to take this breath. And do it any time you feel the first signs of stress.

Technique #2

The Basic Centering Technique

Purpose:

To quickly get to a level where you are one with the Universal Energy, for any benefit you desire.

Application:

Practice the Basic Centering Technique until you feel a very deep level of relaxation and a sense of oneness with the Universe.[1] After that, use the Basic Centering Technique to enter a centered state before doing any of the other techniques in the book.

Procedure:

While you are seated with your feet flat on the ground, touch the thumbs and the forefingers of each hand together lightly, palms comfortably toward your face (see the diagram on page 43). If a position similar to this is more comfortable, feel free to use it. Take a full, deep breath through your mouth and exhale to release excess tension. Now breathe deeply through your nose (you can use your mouth if necessary), first filling your diaphragm with air (see the Perfect Breath Technique) and then your upper lungs by "rolling" the air in to a silent count of three. Hold your breath for a count of one and release it through your mouth (or your nose, if you prefer) to a count of three. Repeat the process to a count of five, holding for a count of two and releasing to a

---

[1] I know the concept of oneness with the Universe sounds like quite an accomplishment, but if it helps, think of it as an all-convincing sense of calm.

count of five. Take a third slow deep breath to a count of seven, hold for a count of three and release it to a count of seven. After this (when you have practiced enough) you will be centered.

Whenever you desire to leave this centered state, tell yourself mentally that you will count from one to five and open your eyes at the count of five, feeling alive, alert, refreshed, and happy. Then count yourself out of this state from one to five.

How it works:

By touching your fingers together and facing your palms up, you are creating a closed field of energy that recycles itself. Touching your fingers together also triggers your body and mind, reminding your entire system to relax and preparing you for what you are going to do. Three deep rolling breaths relaxes you enough that you'll eventually be able to center yourself on command. Besides being a very relaxing technique by itself, taking three breaths also works as a trigger, conditioning your body and mind to immediately relax and enter your level of centeredness. You will be trained to naturally respond to the trigger of the deep breaths by "remembering" the feeling you get when centered. You will begin to reproduce that feeling as soon as you take the first breath.

Additional comments:

If you still feel tension after the third breath, keep breathing deeply until you are relaxed. If you ever feel dizzy, stop, wait a few minutes, and try again. It is natural to feel a bit unusual when you start these techniques, but these feelings will subside with practice. After you get a feel for the counting, try not to count but to estimate the time instead. This may help you get centered more easily. After counting yourself out of the centered state from one to five, relax and enjoy what you feel for a few moments before moving around.

Position for the Basic Centering Technique.

Relax, You're Already Perfect

Lesson II

Find God:
Look In The Mirror

"Why become a Buddhist, when you can become a Buddha?"

Lama Surya Das

Re-discovering who you really are, the whole you, is an enlightening experience. We are spiritual beings incarnated in our present physical forms. To some, this may not sound new, but how many people are actually connected and centered and realize they are using their physical bodies solely to experience the physical world? Just as we have the sense of taste to fully experience food, we have our entire physical being in order for us and God (within us) to fully experience the physical dimension.

The Universe is perfect, and as God's creations, so are we. To better understand how we can be perfect when we seem so fragile, ignorant, vulnerable, and sometimes even savage, we will again chip away at what we are not. By comparison, we will remember more of what we really are. We may also be able to suggest answers to questions that have perplexed our greatest thinkers throughout history, such as:

What is the nature of human existence?

Why were we created?

Do we really have free will?

As in the first lesson, the best way to benefit from this lesson is to temporarily suspend your disbeliefs or preconceptions. Allow for the possibility that we are part of God and, as such, perfect spiritual beings. By accepting this certain things may begin to make sense to you. When you connect with the Universe, these things will *feel* right as well.

Myth: "Nobody's perfect."

> *"Be ye therefore perfect, even as your Father which in heaven is perfect."*
>
> *Matthew V*

Spiritual perfection exists intrinsically within everything. For experiential purposes, everyone in this dimension is created perfectly. Labeling ourselves and our experiences as good or bad does not change the perfect process of re-discovery. Experiences are neither good nor bad. They are only experiences.

The concept of humanity as flawed is a rationalization created by the human ego to explain what we don't understand in this world. The need to understand everything is a quality of the ego of little benefit to us while we are on earth. In fact, the only benefit of the *ego* is to keep us in the illusion of darkness until we are ready to see the light.

In therapeutic sessions, it becomes apparent that most people who embrace the "nobody's perfect" myth are making excuses for humankind (and of course, themselves). They don't feel capable of accepting the responsibility that goes with believing they are powerful enough to affect their own lives, much less the physical world.

When God created humankind, God created perfection. We always were and always will be perfect.[1] Everything we do is perfect. Any way we decide to experience this dimension is perfect. Forget, for the time being, conventional notions of "right and wrong" or "fallibility." To take away from the perfection of humanity would be to doubt the perfection of the Universal Intelligence. How could God be perfect and create something that was not? God is not concerned about our questioning

---

[1] Some people believe that we have the *potential* for perfection and that attaining it is our goal. If these people get comfort from this belief, wonderful. However, understanding ourselves as spiritually perfect *now* frees us from worry, self-doubt, insecurity, and fear. These are limitations and creations of the human mind manifested from a disconnection to our true spiritual nature as one with God.

ourselves, and such doubts would not cause the Almighty a problem. By not being aware of our ethereal reality, we would not be conscious of our fantastic creative abilities and thereby limit our potential to achieve true happiness while in this existence. Most of us are too caught up in what happens in the day-to-day physical world, forgetting that we are so much more than bodies.

Some of us worry about whether our favorite soap opera star will leave the show, and we watch the news to hear about the pain and tragedy that others experience. Then we go to sleep, dream about winning the lottery, and wake up the next day only to do it all over again. It seems *we tiptoe through life hoping to make it safely to death without causing too much trouble!* Do you really believe that this is why God created us? Is this God's perfection at work? There's nothing wrong with watching TV or anything else for that matter, but we can truly appreciate all human experiences in every moment we dwell in this dimension, if we are awake spiritually and realize who we are. The physical world is all there is for those who are asleep.

"But I don't feel perfect."

Some of the most difficult questions I've ever been asked are: If we are one with God, then why wouldn't God have created us with that thought to begin with? What is the purpose of not knowing? Why don't we feel perfect?

I meditated upon these questions for two decades before I was ready to see the answer.

Before we are born, we choose to exist and decide how best to help ourselves and the One Spirit in the process of re-discovery. This is because each individual soul develops as it wishes, while assisting all other souls in their journey. All are experiencing and gaining more of an understanding of the nature of Love. We choose who we will be and to whom we will be born, to best serve that purpose.

We also choose to experience "transformational amnesia," to temporarily forget our spiritual consciousness in order to adjust to the physical world and allow us "real" physical experiences. If we knew we were invulnerable spiritual beings, the effects of these physical experiences would have little or no significance for us. We would know they were not real.

Imagine that you are a passenger on a flight during a severe storm.

The plane is shaking and you see lightning all around you. The "fasten seat belt" sign is illuminated and you start to get frightened. There's a large blast of thunder nearby, and the lights go out inside the cabin. People scream while the aircraft is bouncing up and down like a toy, feeling as if it could break apart at any second. Babies are crying and, as you look around, you can barely make out some people praying in the dark. Your heart beats faster, you start to sweat, your breath shortens, and panic becomes a possibility. You are terrified, and understandably so. No one is telling you anything, and you wonder if the pilots are in control.

Suddenly, the plane calms down and the cabin lights come back on as you hear an announcement; "Ladies and gentlemen, this is your captain speaking. We are out of the storm now and it should be pretty smooth for the duration of the flight." Some passengers applaud, and you're overwhelmed with relief.

What if you were watching a movie of yourself in this situation and knew the ending? Would you have been as scared? What if you *knew* during this predicament that everything would be OK? Would you have had the same emotional experience? Of course not. You needed to live through it without knowing so you could gain a very "real" experience. If you knew what would happen before it happened, it wouldn't feel real.

This is the same with our entire physical existence. Before we are born, we choose to forget who we are so we can get the most out of what is available for us to experience. We're in this world to experience all life's situations as *"reality,"* so we can eventually know ourselves wholly, body, mind, and spirit, *as Love.*

If you realize you are here as a spiritual being, that suggests you've had enough physical experiences to begin to awaken. You start to re-member who you are and why you came here. You lose the feeling of isolation and "re-member" yourself as part of the One Spirit. When and if this happens, you are ready to experience a new perspective on life. You either experience it firsthand or by using your memory, knowing you are a spiritual being inside a physical body. You then begin to realize, as psychologist Frances Vaughan says, "I *have* thoughts, feelings, and sensations, but I *am not* my thoughts, feelings or sensations."

Because we must first forget, most of us get caught up in the "reality" of what we think we see and have a difficult time remembering who we really are. Until we begin to awaken, we remain blind to the perfect process. Since you are reading this book, odds are you're awake, or are beginning to awaken, and are becoming aware that the Higher Intelligence is within and all around you, regardless of what you think you see.

The Universe created this entire process of re-discovery and it is perfect. As part of this process we, in this physical form, play our roles perfectly, *whether we realize and understand it or not.*

Myth: "I'm only human."

> *"What you are shouts so loudly that I cannot hear what you say."*
>
> Ralph Waldo Emerson

The "I'm only human" myth is another common excuse for people who do not feel in control of their lives. You *are* human, but you're not *only* human. If you look past the carbon, nitrogen, oxygen, and the other components of your physical body, you start to remember you are made of energy and not a body at all. This is the same energy that exists in all living things and envelops the Universe. If you see yourself only as a physical being, you reduce everything that humankind truly is to robot-like appliances with no purpose other than to exist until they no longer work. This type of thinking is exactly what Sir Isaac Newton and most physicists and scientists who followed him believed: If things could not be observed and explained by the Scientific Method, they simply did not exist. The human body can be measured with many instruments to tell us where everything is located and how things work. Everything, that is, except for the soul, which can't be found by any man-made instrument. Thus, some closed-minded people continue to believe that the soul does not exist.

Thomas Edison said, *"Our mind is like the wireless operator. It uses right or wrong thought currents. If we are not in tune with the infinite or to higher vibrations, failure is the result."* This is the brilliant scientist's description of the importance of "tuning" our essence, or energy, into God's energy by centering. It is amazing how many scientists do believe in the Almighty, despite an inability to prove God's existence. It seems that the feelings many of us share about the existence of the Higher Intelligence are stronger than any mortal evidence. Results offer the best proof.

After you repeatedly experience the results of believing, you may need no further proof, finally allowing yourself to relax and *feel* the perfection of the Universe within you. Until that time, God is a mystery — and so then, is your life.

Instead of denying the possibility of what we cannot know at a given time, accept for now the mysterious aspects of existence. Accepting mystery is truly empowering and a sign of wisdom. This is part of living the perfect process as an awakened being. By accepting and understanding what *not knowing* is, this process will eventually bring us the experience of *knowing*. I have seen and felt the results of the energy of the Universe. You can too, if you are able to overcome the current limited physical abilities of the human (individual) mind and tap into the limitless possibilities of the Universal Mind. Once you do this and let God's presence be felt within you, you will know you are a perfect creation.

Myth: "I'll leave it up to fate."

> "God is our Creator. God made us in [God's] image and likeness. Therefore we are creators."
>
> Dorothy Day

It would be difficult to find a less empowering myth than one that implies the existence of fate. We are the manifestations of the Spiritual Energy in this physical form. Through that power, we create our experiences as we desire — consciously or not. If God had no reason to experience the physical world through our creative abilities, we wouldn't have those abilities and we wouldn't be here.

Truth: Everything created by God has purpose

Unless God likes watching re-runs, the Universal Intelligence enjoys our physical experiences *now*, as we create them. It's the purpose of our existence in this dimension for the Universal Spirit to benefit from our bodily experiences, just as we use our own physical senses to experience what is around us. The many different situations we choose to create helps us all remember Love. Therefore, since we are co-creators with the Universe and our lives are not following the path of fate, we are empowered to create our lives through the potential of our own abilities.

Free will

If there were no pre-planned course for our lives, we would be able to direct and control what happens to us through the exercise of free will. This is the truth. Our free will allows us to make choices about what we do, how we act, which roads we take, and what we perceive and believe. More precisely, our free will lets us choose what to remember about ourselves, what type of life experience we have, and *when* to remember who we really are. It doesn't matter to the Universe what choices we make — it matters only to us when we are here on earth. While we all end up as Love, our choices remain important because we don't have to sleep through this wonderful gift of a physical life.

Another thought about free will: You are free to challenge, with an open mind, everything you read and everything you've ever heard. Just as *challenge* is a beneficial process of growth, *controversy* for the sole purpose of endless debate can stunt your growth and limit your potential for happiness. Your free will has the choice to look for enlightenment and peace or to look for hollow controversy. Either way, *you will find what you look for.*

Now we come to a most challenging question. If everything we are and do is perfect, how do you explain murder, starvation, hate, and the perpetuation of all other inhumane atrocities that we seem to indiscriminately dole out? Let's not confuse the perfection of the Universe with what, on the surface, seems to be mistakes. There is perfection even in making "mistakes." *It is part of the perfect process.* That's how we experience, grow, define, and re-discover who we really are. "Bad" choices are essential to free will and are purposeful. Nothing human is alien to perfection.

A good or bad apple is still an apple. Nothing can change its essence. We are one with God. There is spiritual perfection within each of us, and nothing we say or do can change who we really are.

Judgments of right and wrong and good and bad, which most of us make, about life's situations are spiritually irrelevant. We are here to experience physical life, and we do that perfectly, to have unique individual experiences, and to share these experiences with the Universe. All experiences help us to know Love. We are free to view the world as we wish; to enjoy our lives or live in misery. Either way, however, assists all souls in the re-discovery of Love for the One Spirit.

The penalties of "bad" choices

Although we seem to perpetuate and repeat many painful experiences without learning from them, in actuality each experience anyone has in life is new and valuable to us all. The only penalty for what we call a mistake is that we delay the awareness of the truth that there are no mistakes from a spiritual perspective. This penalty is created and imposed by us. If you believe yourself capable of mistakes, you live in fear of making them, always serving as judge and jury for your every action and constantly sentencing yourself to self-condemnation. You imprison yourself with unhappiness.

God does not punish — only we punish ourselves. When we do something against our inner truth, we think we lose. We actually just re-discover more of who we really are by experiencing more of who we are not. Anything we experience in our lives is purposeful as part of the perfect process of re-discovery. But we needn't go through an entire life unhappy because of choices that always seem to turn out wrong.

The choice is up to you

As creators of our lives, the choices we make determine who we are and are important to us now. If we make "spiritually loving" choices, we create the potential for the greatest amount of happiness. It seems difficult to make the most beneficial choices for ourselves and which paths to take. Thankfully, you do not have to guess.

There are a few ways to know if your choices will bring you happiness. First, practice centering (see the Basic Centering Technique on page 41) and allowing yourself to feel and listen to your emotions while in a centered state. If, after enough practice, something feels good in that state of connectedness, it is *God*, not *good*, that you feel. When you listen to this presence by following your heart, you act in harmony with the Universe. The Universe then backs you up with its energy. With all that power behind you, you reap extraordinary rewards.

Let me give you a personal example. Right after I decided to go to graduate school to become a therapist, I was centered and received the "inspiration" to develop a company to help people get into the retail food industry. My wife and I decided to be consultants. We had discussed this in the past (she had been in the business for many years), but had never proceeded with the idea because we knew of no other company, beside franchises, that was doing what we wanted to do. We felt some franchises were not providing people with a fair deal, charging too much for what they were offering franchisees, and then taking royalties "to boot." We believed our ideas could help, but figured the type of business we had in mind must either be too difficult or not worth it. If it were profitable, why wasn't anyone else doing it? While centered, I felt it was the best thing to do at that time, and that it would help us financially while I developed my true spiritual purpose. So I programmed (*i.e.* centered) myself and created the success[2] in which the Universe assisted me. The business did exactly what I programmed it to do. *When you are following your true purpose in this life, the Universe backs you up.*

In no time, we were running a nearly million-dollar-a-year consulting business. By providing people an alternative to buying a franchised business, we saved them tremendous amounts of money. We also brought in nearly three times the income I had made in the family business. The best part was that once I worked hard to set the business up, I was able to hire and train someone to do most of the legwork, which left me the time to develop and pursue my true calling. Perfect! I thank God for giving me the free choice to open my eyes to the information that aided in actualizing my purpose. Our ability to start the retail food consulting business had always been there but had not been brought into effect until I was inspired by *feeling* it was the right time to do so.

When you begin to remember who you really are and live your soul's purpose (Lesson V), you are functioning as part of the Universe instead of in isolation. In a centered state, you will *desire* to follow the universal purpose (helping yourself and others re-discover themselves as Love) for your happiness and that of your brothers and sisters. In this case, the Universe has no choice but to back you up. You will have the energy of everything around you to help, and you will be able to create miracles. Only by operating out of a centered state will you remain an individual and struggle to find out who you really are and see the truth.

Everyone makes choices in his or her life. I have made great choices and I've made choices I later wished I hadn't. The common denominator of the "better" choices is that all were made in a centered, meditative state. They all felt right at that level of mind. Only I could judge

---

[2] Lesson VI explains how to do this.

these choices and decide if they were right for me, and I made my decisions by determining if my results helped me become the person I felt I had the potential to be. Only we can realize what the best choices are for ourselves. No one can choose for another.

Application: Choose with the Universe

The next time you have to make a difficult decision, close your eyes and clear your mind. Ask the Universe for help. Connect with God to help you reveal the answer. The answers to all your questions are always there within you.

Center yourself using the Basic Centering Technique and ask the Universe a question. "Listen" to your emotions and allow them to let you feel the correct answer. (The next lesson helps you interpret those feelings.) Do not read too much into these feelings except to let them tell you if what you are asking feels right for you. Don't be surprised when you begin to get answers. Many times when you are centered, the exact information you are seeking just "pops" into your mind. Or you will see a sign telling you how to proceed.

Practice the "Success Tuning Technique" at the end of this lesson to develop your decision-making abilities.

Judging others' choices

Judging others' choices is not God-like. Everything anyone does gives an experience to all. That's why we don't have to each experience everything first-hand. If anyone does something, we all do. Judging others by what we believe is right or wrong makes the assumption that we know better than the people we judge. We know very little about what is best for other peoples' purposes. We can only decide what's best for ourselves.

"Judge not what I was, nor what I am, but what I will have become." I wrote this a long time ago after a meditation but didn't understand it until years later. It was through a direct connection with my Higher Self, and I knew I would understand when I was ready. Let's look at the parts of the statement separately.

"Judge not what I was...." Certainly there is no reason to judge the past, since most of us are no longer in it. (For those of you who do live in the past, realize there is no future in it!) As far as the second part goes, "...nor what I am...," why judge what I am today since I will be different tomorrow. Judging me today will only deplete your energy (and mine if I judge myself.)

These two lines were not difficult for me to understand. It was the last line ("...but what I will have become.") I found the most revealing. Not what I was, not what I am, but what I will have become. This seemed paradoxical. No one can judge what someone will have *become* because we are becoming something new every moment until we die. Then we will have *been* (physically). Because the statement is paradoxical, the meaning I received years later was, simply stated, "God does not need to judge; you do not need to judge — anyone, ever."

Throughout your life, people have judged you and you have judged them. As you created and perpetuated judgment, you also created and perpetuated an illusory feeling of separation between you and those around you. This feeling of separation has led to more unhappiness in your life than you can imagine. You are better than no one and no one is better than you. To help you see the goodness (Godness) in others, try this exercise:

Application: Finding God in others

When you wake up, tell yourself that you will look for God in every person you see and meet today. I used to get angry with bad drivers (that is, people who didn't drive the way I wanted them to). When someone cut me off or was inconsiderate, I became aggressive and made sure they knew I wasn't happy. It's amazing that I never got into a fist fight because of my attitude. Now, if a driver does something thoughtless, I've conditioned myself to think, "This is my brother (or sister); this is God. I choose to love this person the best I can." This simple viewpoint has prevented me from getting as angry while driving. I actually apologize to the other driver, even when I believe he or she was at fault. The best thing is that I feel good about myself afterward. I know it is the right thing for me.

When you look at people non-judgmentally, as if they were God, you see them in a totally different light. Sometimes I want to just go up and hug a stranger. But since I prefer not to get arrested, I merely admire them from afar. It's a wonderful, peaceful feeling to look at others this way.

Myth: "There are sinners among us."

"Neither hath this man sinned, nor his parents: but the works of God should be manifest in him."
John 9:1-3, King James Version

Even what appears to some people as sinning is part of the perfect process. As discussed in the previous lesson, there are no sins in God's eyes since this would suggest that God is judging and deciding what right and wrong is for you. You are one with God and *you* must find out who you are by experiencing what you believe right and wrong is for *you*. Sinning would propose mistakes, and there are none.

Imagine how circumscribed our lives would be if we did only the "socially correct" thing all the time. To be sure, we would be limiting our experiences, but even more important we would never be able to know what Love is. This can only be known by comparison. The concept of sinning was created by people who insisted others believe what they believed, convincing them that if they did not, they would spend an eternity in hell.

Truth: We are all equally perfect

Each of us has been perfectly created to play his or her part in the process of re-discovery. Each person helps re-discover Love through his or her distinct experiences. Through this process, we remember we are all one. Find your own truths, without fear of making mistakes or sinning. Listen to others, but decide for yourself. Eventually, you'll decide that what you do and think is who you are. When you are awakened to your spiritual reality, you'll only do and think from a perspective of Love, and you'll be truly happy as a result. You'll then also see how everyone is as equally remarkable as you.

Accountability for your actions

You may ask, "If we are capable of free will and can do as we please, without judgment from God, how can we be accountable for what we do?"

This may surprise a lot of people, but we do not have to be accountable to anyone else for what we do. If you break the law, you choose to take the chance of going to jail. This does not suggest a spiritual right or wrong, but only that there are controls society sets up to prevent chaos. If you choose to violate those controls, your free will may land you in trouble. Not spiritual trouble: only practical, physical trouble. We are accountable only to ourselves.

We owe ourselves the chance to become all we can be, to realize our fullest possibilities. The choices we make that prevent this limit our potential for true happiness.

I suggest to people that even though God doesn't hold them accountable for how they live, they should nevertheless live a spiritually loving life for their own benefit. A few clients have asked if they would be rewarded by God for living a more loving life than those who don't, remarking this would suggest preferential treatment. While no one is more worthy than another, and it doesn't matter to God what type of life experience you create, *there are rewards for those who love.* God does not give these rewards to you, however. They are inherent in you, and when you come to know yourself as one with the Universe, you tap into the power that is available to move mountains. *You have the creative power of God within you!* You can create anything you truly desire. When I centered myself and received the inspiration to pursue the consulting business, I also received many ideas about how to proceed. My success was a sign that pursuing that business was right for me at that time. I created this "success" by connecting with my Higher Self after deciding to move in the best direction to help myself and others re-discover themselves as Love. The consulting business was the right bridge to keep my family financially stable so I could cross over into a more purposeful existence. I created my own rewards by using more of my natural spiritual abilities (which some people call psychic abilities).

If you choose to ignore your spiritual nature, that's OK, but you will not know yourself as the incredible being you really are — at least not in this lifetime. This concept is one that should by now be familiar to you. You can do whatever you choose with your life. It is your free will. God gave us all opportunities for growth and happiness in our lives. Your free will decides if you take advantage of these opportunities. Your deepest, most desirable dreams can be attained if you act *now* and follow a conscious spiritual life to reach your potential for happiness. Why wait?

Myth: "I guess I just have to pay my karmic debts."

The client who expressed this felt he was paying for his past. He believed he was destined to suffer to atone for certain misdeeds he had performed in the past. Some extend this imagined "debt" to past lives. I am really quite tired of hearing people say they have to suffer for anything. We are the creators of our own suffering. If you believe God to be the cause of your suffering, it is *you* that brings power to that thought. Due to cause-and-effect, you would be *causing* with your own power, the *effect* of your own suffering. God is powerful. You, too, are powerful, and you can use this power any way you wish, including remaining a victim of the past.

The concept of "karma" is not well understood by most people. Although there is nothing that you have to pay anyone, karma does exist in a different sense. You *do* reap what you sow, and certain habits derive from behaviors one's parents sowed. But what you sow is your choice, and how you reap its effects can be changed with your own creative abilities. If you act out of hatred, you will most likely believe yourself worthy of punishment. If you realize that there are no spiritual repercussions to something you may have done in this or a prior life, you can remove the idea of indebtedness (along with your suffering) and live in Love.

The concept of reaping what we sow is the same as getting what you give, and it is quite simple. If you have only Love within you, Love is all you can give. In turn, people will give back what you give them. Furthermore, you can receive only what you are capable of owning, which is more of what you already have inside. If you do something nice for others, they will usually thank you by doing something nice for you. If you hurt them, they may strike back. No right or wrong is involved; it's just a simple physical result of your actions.

First, decide who you want to be and then be that person *today* by acting out of Love. You'll find that most people around you feel, or would like to feel, the same. They'll be attracted to you, helping you to experience more of yourself through them (Lesson IX). Those in a different place than you will probably fade from your life. Remember who you are, live as Love, and your entire life experience will change. Create a cycle of Love. This is karma. No one needs to be unhappy for a lifetime.

Myth: "Emotions make us human."

When I asked the person who said this to explain her meaning, she realized she often felt too emotional and out of control. Why do you think God created emotions? Anything created by God is perfect, and emotions are part of that perfection. Still, too many let emotions control them instead of understanding their purpose. Before we look at a few specific emotions, think about this; our emotions are a great asset, given to us by the Universal Intelligence to help us decide what feels pleasurable or painful. They guide us during our journey to remember our true selves as Love — the only real emotion. When we listen to our emotions, we find the key to understanding the truth for us. If we are not awakened, emotions can be misinterpreted. When misunderstood, they can be detrimental to our happiness. This relates to the concept of free will. We can *choose* to believe anything we want. Change our viewpoints about certain events and the emotions we feel will change as well.[3]

Many people allow their emotions to be determined by past experience. The past is of great value if we allow ourselves to benefit from the experience. We have the power to change our feelings about the past, understand those feelings, or even to relive the past in our minds.

Application: Connect the past and present

If possible, visit a place you haven't seen in a long time — maybe a neighborhood you grew up in or a school you attended. Whatever you see, understand how it was, and still is, part of you, bringing the past and present together for that moment. Whatever you see was created by God (through humanity) and is perfect. If you feel a pleasurable emotion, immerse yourself in the feeling and enjoy the experience without thinking. If you experience an unpleasant feeling from a memory, take a few deep breaths and repeat, "There is and always was a purpose to everything. I am a perfect creation: God is in me, always has been, always will be."

All humans are emotional beings but some are more ready than others are to experience the full power of emotions. Through the unconscious use of defense mechanisms, some choose to not allow themselves

---

[3] We choose how to react to most situations, releasing hormones in our bodies that make us feel certain ways.

to feel as much pain and sorrow as others. Others may turn to addictions, such as drugs or overeating, to distract from their perceived reality. These people may succeed in this, but they are limiting their capacity for Love, which is why God created the "bad" emotions.

Let's now take a look at some of our emotions and their meaning in our lives, focusing on a few that cause people to feel less than perfect.

Fear: We have been afraid of dying, of being injured, and of being alone since we were created. We conjure up a seemingly endless list of phobias and anxieties. In the perfect process of re-discovery, the Universal Intelligence created fear so we could protect ourselves and survive. In this sense, fear is born out of Love — the love of life. All human emotions are born out of Love for one purpose or another.

Another purpose for fear is to know when we no longer fear. As we experience fear, we prepare ourselves for the experience of knowing blissful peace in its absence. The absence of fear suggests the presence of true Love. All emotions serve this purpose. We need not fear fear itself, but we do need to understand its purpose. When we are fearful, we can be conscious of why we are experiencing it at that time. If you feel fearful, put it in perspective. Allow yourself to experience it and understand it, and then remove that feeling by centering yourself. There is no better opportunity to feel peace than right after we feel fear. We can't know peace without it, but we do not have to live in fear. Fear is an illusion of the physical world created to know Love, the only eternal emotion. Eventually, we no longer need to fear, and it ceases to exist.

> "...and fear shall be known no more, and sorrow and sighing shall flee away."
>
> *Isaiah 35:10*

Hatred: Why do you think God created hatred? If you answered, "so we can know what Love is not," congratulations. Hate is a powerful emotion that is part of the total human experience. You would choose feeling hatred over feeling nothing since not feeling anything deprives you of your human nature and the ability to know Love.

What are some of the things we hate? Prejudice? Violence? Human suffering? Because the reason for all emotions is to help us know Love, we must accept hatred as part of the perfect process. However, after we experience it and allow it to serve its purpose, we can move past hatred (and other "bad" emotional experiences) because the emotion is no longer needed. It is our free will that decides if we will realize emotions for what they are and move past them. Free will is part of our mind, which chooses and creates our realities. Some people live in the "reality" of hatred. Why dwell in only one emotion and forget its purpose?

Let's look at hatred in its most powerful expression and see how the magic of God works. Hitler hated Jews, and his passion drove him to try to destroy the Jewish people. Hitler was not centered. Instead, he lived with a limited range of emotions predominated by hatred, fear, and an insatiable quest for power. He was never able to understand the purpose behind those emotions. He chose instead to live *in* those emotions, and so, to live in the physical world only. (He chose the Jewish people on whom to act out his feelings.) In his conscious mind, he was a perfect, powerful, superior being. But because he was not centered, this was not the loving, unifying feeling of power that God created for us to feel through love for our fellow human beings; it was hatred in disguise. His self-conceived ideas, unconsciously created out of fear of inferiority, compelled him to prove himself superior.

How can what Hitler did be considered anything less than blasphemy? The answer, that there is no right and wrong in God's eyes, didn't diminish my personal and painful feelings about the horrors of the holocaust. I believed I felt as much hatred toward him as he did toward the Jewish people. I even wondered if this hatred made me comparable to him. It took quite some time before I was able to understand and move past those feelings of hatred. I had a lot of confusing thoughts until an answer came to me when I was ready.

From a human perspective, Hitler was an abomination, seemingly destroying what God created to satisfy his personal addiction to power. From a physical perspective, humanity suffered at the hands of a madman. Anything we as a people had to do to stop him was necessary, because our efforts said something about who we were and in what we believed. Our feelings about him are very important, so we remember more of what Love is not. I later understood that my hatred was derived from my love of humanity. It allowed me to know more of what I stood for; to know more of who I was.

Humanity, too, discovered, to some degree, much about itself from this historical event. As a whole, we developed into more of what we were by experiencing something we were not. Hitler's actions were formed by the belief systems of many people's conscious and unconscious collective minds, which resulted in the holocaust. Many felt that certain people were not equal to them (some still do). It was a time in human history when we had to make a choice. We had to decide if what Hitler was doing felt like Love to us. When most people listened to their emotions and decided that what he was doing felt "wrong," the means to end his reign was created. We re-discover more about the nature of Love by examples such as this. If we had made a different choice and allowed Hitler to continue his butchery, we would have had to re-experience our pain again and again until we found the truth. The truth is Love. Everything that happens moves us in Love's direction.

What about those who died in the holocaust? Surely, they suffered? Remember, there is no right or wrong, nor judgment or punishment, from a spiritual perspective. There is also no death in a spiritual sense (Lesson VII). Imagine, if you can, that all the souls whose bodies died at Hitler's hands are now either reborn or waiting for their loved ones so they can re-unite with the Universal Spirit before continuing their journey. Their passing, albeit a painful physical existence for all involved, helped to move humanity in the direction of Love. Therefore, their passing was for their own eternal benefit as well, since we are all the same single spiritual presence.

We need not repeat history, nor should we thank Hitler for the experience. Thank only God for giving us the ability to create all experiences for our self-discovery. We need only remember that everything that happens has purpose and that we should always look at the big picture. Let us thank all souls whose loss in this physical existence helps humanity remember more of the nature of Love.

Love: This emotion will be discussed in depth in the next lesson. For now, remember that it is the only true emotion. Love is the essence of the Universe. All other emotions exist in this physical dimension so we can know the reality of Love.

Guilt: I remember once believing that guilt was a wasted emotion. People usually feel guilty about doing, saying, or believing things they were told were wrong. In this case it really is a waste, because unnecessary guilt limits our potential for happiness. We should remember what we were told but listen to our hearts to decide if the information describes who we are or want to be. Unfortunately, because it is such a strong emotion, guilt sometimes gets in the way of our inner truth. With a little help from fear and anxiety, guilt keeps us trapped and asleep. To break out, you may have to think it possible that everything you were told by your parents, clergy, teachers, and peers might be completely wrong for you. If you're able to at least accept this as a possibility, you're on your way. If not, you'll be trapped until you awaken.

Like all emotions, there is a place for guilt. A *centered* spiritual being, one who has moved past her limiting beliefs, will feel guilty doing something that goes against who she is or wants to be. As a youth I got caught up with gambling and decided, along with a couple of friends, to become a bookie. We took bets from friends, paid off when they won, and collected when they lost. Because they almost always lost, we made a ton of money. I remember making about $10,000 one week. We did this for a summer, and I felt guilty. I was taking advantage of my friends. As we watched, some of these friends lost everything. I told my "business associates" how I felt and received the expected rationalization: "If they don't bet with us, they'll do it with someone else."

I still felt guilty, and after someone I knew was arrested for bookmaking, I felt fearful as well. I decided these feelings were telling me that being a bookie was wrong. It was not a matter of being right or wrong in the eyes of God. It was only that being a bookie was not who I wanted to be and, therefore, not right for me. So I quit, and my associates continued for years, never getting caught. To this day one still doesn't understand why I quit. His path was different than mine, and I knew that my calling was not to be a bookie because it didn't feel like Love to me. Eventually, my friend gave up his "business" due to a lack of customers. He says he has no regrets. But by seeing and listening to him then and now, I believe he was both guilty and unhappy, even though his professed belief system told him the happiness of others was not something he needed to be concerned with. He was unaware that his actions caused a disconnection with others that led to his own unhappiness. After reading this I hope he'll see a purpose to that unhappiness and remember his true nature of Love and oneness with all.

If we are willing to listen to examples such as this (and are not imprisoned by past belief systems), our emotions will work *for* us, and we can remember more about who we are.

Application: How do you feel about your life?

Do you feel guilty and/or unhappy, or do you simply feel you could be happier? If so, this could be the result of something you are doing in your life that doesn't describe your true nature. Center yourself, think about a particular aspect of your life, and listen to the message in your emotion. Does your thought feel like Love, or does it create dissonance? If it doesn't feel like Love, spend a few moments remembering how you began what you are doing. What were you told and what experiences did you have to reinforce this limitation? If what you do holds you back in some way, stop doing it and test the emotional response again while centered. It is your choice how you act. It is up to you to use your emotions as guides. That is their true purpose.

Affirmations

Affirmations help you "program" what you wish to manifest in the physical world. While you are in a centered state, repeat silently any or all of the following statements for your benefit.

"I am part of God and God is within me. I have only to close, then open, my eyes and see."

"It is my free will to choose how I feel about anything and anyone. I feel what I choose to feel."

"When I accept 'bad' things as part of the perfect process of the Universe, I am truly empowered."

"I am one with all humanity. I am completely loving and accepting of everyone."

"I am one with the Universe; I am a perfect creation."

Lesson II summary:

Resist the temptation to judge humanity by what we say or do. Our perfection lies within our ability to make choices and experience the physical dimension to re-discover the reality of Love for the One Spirit.

As we start to remember we are a perfect creation, we move closer to Love. We remember that we are Divine, indestructible, and totally loving in our natural state. Once remembered, we realize we have the power to consciously continue God's work as co-creators of the world and make it a happier place.

We souls are like rivers, flowing purposefully in a journey to eventually meet in an ocean of Love. In this ocean, we are united as One Spirit.

Our rivers flow not outward but inward. This is how we re-discover our true nature, and this is how we find God. As it is written in the Bible, "The kingdom of heaven is within us."

Are you ready to accept the reality that you are greater than you could have ever imagined?

Relax, You're Already Perfect

Technique #3

The Success Tuning Technique

Purpose:

To create an "in-the-moment" spiritual experience similar to the feeling of being truly "on" or "present" occasionally experienced during a peak performance in sports. The Success Tuning Technique allows you to tune into a past successful connection with the Universe and bring that feeling with you to create a new experience. This technique helps you more consciously enjoy a physical experience, and to *feel* what a beneficial direction or decision is for you, wherever and whenever you desire.

Application:

Use this technique whenever you need to ask questions (in a centered state) and desire to feel the answers. It can also be used in a waking state any time you have to make a decision and for many physical activities.

Procedure:

Center yourself with the Basic Centering Technique (on page 41). Once centered, feel the presence of God within you. This feeling is one of joy, security, peace, compassion, wisdom, and Love. Practice the centering process until you begin to experience this wonderful feeling of being one with the Universe as soon as you take your third deep breath. Once you master this, you'll feel only the energy of Love in this state. When you do, repeat silently "I feel the power of the Universe," or any other powerful affirmation from this book or another source. Once satisfied that you can recreate this feeling on command, you are ready to "tune into" the power of Love and ask questions. Center yourself, repeat whatever affirmation you "programmed" and ask any question. Then clear your mind, and wait for the answer, which will eventually "pop" in. If it feels like Love, you're on the right track. You can even think of a possible answer and examine, or test, the feelings associated with it. Is it the same loving feeling as before? If so, then it is the most spiritually beneficial answer for you and everyone involved. If it is not the best answer, you'll experience a disconnection that does not feel like Love, and you will be centered no longer. If this happens, it is not the most advantageous answer. Repeat the centering process and wait for, or think about, the answer that feels the same as Love.

For a physical activity (or any other activity that you wish to bring about a greater possibility of success), center yourself, repeat your powerful affirmation, and tune into a past successful physical effort. Try to recreate the feelings you had at the time as best you can. Bring in all the senses. Now take that successful feeling with you in your current activity.

How it works:

Once you have the ability to tune into Love, you can ask questions or check your answers in a centered state and remember the feeling of rightness for you as it was programmed before. By doing this you will always know the loving answer; the one best for you, because it is from the Universal Intelligence. Tuning in for a physical experience helps you do what you are doing to the best of your ability. Programming the affirmation while in the blissful centered state locks in the feeling. It connects the feeling with the affirmation. Whenever you repeat the affirmation, you tap into the powerful feeling you experienced before, which connects you to the state of mind previously experienced and now wish to repeat.

Additional comments:

If you have an immediate decision to make in your waking state, simply close your eyes, take three deep breaths, repeat your affirmation, and make the best decision you can by listening to your feelings. If you can't take the time to close your eyes and take three deep breaths, simply take a single deep breath, repeat the affirmation, and try to feel the best answer.

Do not try to force an answer you want. Consider trusting this process and letting go. Be ready to accept any answer you feel and act upon it. If you prefer a desired result, this technique will not work. Remain as neutral as possible before entering the centered state. Let it be, and it will happen. If you get an answer that is not accompanied by the feeling of peace and Love, it will not be from your Higher Self and may not work for you in the physical world. Practice the Success Tuning Technique for business, sex, and other physical activities for a reliable in-the-moment feeling of success (see Lesson VI).

Relax, You're Already Perfect

Lesson III

Love Is The Answer (Unconditionally)

What is the nature of God?
God is Love.
What is the purpose of our existence?
To know Love.
How can I know the truth?
Love will tell you the truth.
Who am I?
Love is the answer.

The power of Love is unimaginable. When we remember how to love unconditionally, we allow ourselves to experience what we and God (within us) are really made of. There's no reason why we, as God's creations, cannot remember who we really are. God is everywhere and in everyone, and Love is our true nature.

Think what it would mean to be a completely loving person. There would no longer be a need to judge, question, or doubt any other human being. By adopting a perspective of pure Love, we recognize that *everyone* is a part of God's perfection and equally worthy of receiving our Love and understanding. Once realized, this truth will help bring peace and happiness to all of God's creations.

Becoming more loving not only helps you move closer to your spiritual nature, but also helps you create a happier world for yourself and everyone you touch. It is our innate desire to love one another as we do God, and to understand that the Universal Intelligence *is* true unconditional Love, as are we all in our natural spiritual state.

The spiritual world is a paradise. When you re-discover yourself as Love, you'll realize you live in paradise now. You can taste a bit of that bliss by exploring your creative abilities with the Personal Paradise Technique described at the end of this lesson.

Application: God and your Personal Paradise

Once you spend a little time in your personal paradise, try to sense that God is enjoying this Eden with you. Imagine having a conversation with the Higher Intelligence. Become an observer as well as the creator of this utopia. Use all your "extra" senses to develop your abilities in this dimension. Allow this creation of yours to be as perfect as if a Supreme Intelligence created it. God did.

When you view life through loving eyes, you see the beauty around you more clearly. When you have only Love within you, it is all you can share with another and all you are capable of receiving in return. As you love all other beings unconditionally, you let go of jealousy. You see and connect with the Supreme Intelligence in everything and everyone. Although temporarily split into different forms, we are all one spiritual being. Anything anyone else does will make you proud, as if the other's success was also created by you. In actuality, it was. Here is a personal example of this feeling of oneness.

One day while driving, I was feeling very in touch with my Spiritual Self. I felt as if I belonged to the whole world and it to me. Just then, I heard one of my all-time favorite songs on the radio. I sang along as I always did, but instead of wishing *I* had written the song, I felt I *had* written it. I tried to interpret the meaning of this feeling, and then it became clear: I was feeling a connection to the song's creators and realized they were a part of me. I felt proud of what *we* had accomplished and I was proud to be one with them. This epitomizes the "connectedness" I described earlier. All I needed was to have nothing but Love in me to feel this wonderful connection. By doing this, I could sense all the experiences that anyone else had or was having. Just imagine what this can do to remove the feeling of separation from the spectrum of your human experience. What a revelation!

In the past I had wanted to be a professional musician and realized for the first time that in a way I was. I was living the experience of being a musician through this song. I felt a connection and knew that I didn't need to be a musician or anything else different from what I was at that moment.

For you to experience a similar sensation, try this exercise.

Application: Feeling united

Listen to a song, watch a movie, or read a loved poem. Sit down quietly, close your eyes, center yourself, and repeat, "I am so proud that my brother (or sister) created this beautiful treasure. My brother (or sister) and I are one." Keep saying this phrase until you produce a feeling of connectedness. This feeling is a taste of what it's like to remember you are a spiritual being on earth.

Let us now look at some of the myths that hold people back from remembering and using the magical power of Love.

Myth: "God doesn't love me."

The person who told me this myth was suffering from a disease usually attributed to stress. Her stress we agreed, was the result of a considerable amount of self-doubt she'd felt all her life. She did not believe she was a worthy person in God's eyes. As with all the myths I debunk, she was detrimentally affected by that viewpoint.

To better understand God's concept of unconditional Love, let's look carefully at what this myth suggests. If the love of the Almighty was conditional, it would suggest that God had requirements. If you met certain requirements you would receive love. If not, you wouldn't. This is absurd. God only desires us to experience the human dimension. Unfortunately, some of us live our lives in fear of making mistakes in the Almighty's eyes and miss many opportunities for happiness.

It helps to understand that the Almighty will and does love us as God loves God; we are part of the Universe and the Almighty is within us. Some people believe that if you are not "worthy" you will not be with God when you die. God loves us unconditionally. We all "get to heaven," and heaven is the Love within us all. We can experience heaven on earth by remembering ourselves as true Love. To be more loving is a part of our spiritual journey. As we grow more loving we become more God-like. When we become more God-like, our Love increases.

Myth: "Love comes and goes."

Love is the only reality in the Universe. All else is an illusion. God gave us other emotions only so we can know and express the nature of Love and eventually remember ourselves as totally loving.

Love doesn't just come and go. It is always there within us, waiting to be expressed. Feelings of ecstasy, happiness, and other pleasant emotions are all elements and expressions of Love. This does not mean all the "good" emotions are real and the "bad" ones are not. All emotions are real to us in the physical world, but they are only as real as the physical world itself. As long as we are here, we live in the actuality of all emotions. When we begin to awaken, we eventually remember that we are only Love. This is important to realize so we do not get caught up in any particular emotion besides Love, although everything has a purpose.

Myth: "I am too angry to feel Love."

I've had many clients tell me they feel anger toward someone or some situation. They know it is hurtful to hold on to this feeling but don't know how to release it. They dwell in anger and forget its purpose. Anger helps us experience what Love is not. Actually, anger is an expression of Love; it is derived from a new or previous threat to something we love. Why would we want to deny it?

There are many opportunities to experience the entire range of painful emotions and occurrences in our lifetimes. We all fear, hate, cry, and feel loss and grief. At the time, we wish we did not have to experience these feelings. However, these painful experiences are all part of the perfect process created by the Universe, and we must have these feelings to know Love.

If you feel angry, accept that anger as a natural part of your development. Understand its message, and then let it go.

In Zen Buddhism there is a concept of "dependent co-arising," which states that opposites are necessary to mutually define each other. This is similar to the production of electricity, which requires opposite poles for its generation. However, unlike electricity, which can be produced and maintained only by these opposites, Love is all there is. Its comparative "opposites" are but an illusion in this dimension.

Truth: Anything that doesn't have a purpose ceases to exist

Because Love is the only reality, once we re-discover its true nature, all the comparative illusions are no longer necessary. If this sounds unusual, think of evolution: when something was no longer needed, it became extinct. After we left the sea, we lost our fins. When we no longer needed tails, they disappeared.

We don't have to perpetuate a bad feeling. We don't even have to experience all of life's painful situations ourselves, since many of our brothers and sisters have, or are now, doing so for us. We can experience these feelings vicariously, and there are an infinite number of physical experiences that we desire to create. Desiring many experiences is one reason we have many physical lives[1] so we can see things from alternate perspectives.

Although most of us are unaware of it, we have a remarkable connection to everything and everyone. When people pass from this world, we feel their pain and that of the loved ones left behind. It is the genius of God's design that we are able to experience things and grow. Otherwise, it would be necessary to repeat history over and over again. It is part of the perfect process created by the preeminent genius.

If you are ready to realize that all the physical experiences you have had (and will have) happened so you can know Love, you are ready to step into a different mind frame to remember who you really are. Then when you feel other emotions, you can simply say, "I don't like what I'm feeling, but I understand it and thank the Universe for the experience." After you do this, it is easier to let the unwanted emotional experience go since it will no longer be needed.

Truth: You can break the cycle of suffering through Love

I'm often asked why it is so difficult for people to break their cycles of depression and addiction and to heal themselves physically, emotionally, and spiritually. It is because they wallow in their emotions and situations instead of just experiencing them. People often believe that

---

[1] Reincarnation is discussed in Lesson VII.

the physical world and their emotional reactions to it are out of their control. Some (the Sleepers) also believe that the physical world is all there is. Whatever the reason, these people live a deception that prevents them from moving past their physical conceptions of the world. This deception prevents total happiness. Only after their physical lives are over do they realize that their negative life experience was an illusion they needlessly got caught in — a personal "hell." All suffering is the manifestation of a disconnection between body, mind, and spirit.

Life is a precious gift, and it is a shame to live it in suffering, hatred, depression, and addiction. There may be a place for anger and all other negative emotions in our lives, but it is a very small place. We need only to experience these emotions briefly, understand their purpose for us at the time, and then move on.

Myth: "Hate is the opposite of love."

There is actually no opposite of Love, as Love is all there is. Hate is neither more nor less significant than any other emotion. For now, it is important to remember that we should accept hatred, anger, and all the "negative" emotions as part of the gifts from our creator. These gifts should not be taken lightly, as I again assure you that you'd much rather feel bad than not feel at all. There is no progress in being numb. There is little human experience available to people who ignore or turn off all emotions and live as robots.

Do not be afraid to feel hatred, fear, sorrow, loss, etc. Instead of acting on these feelings, acknowledge and accept them while realizing their true purpose for re-discovery. Sooner or later, the pain and fear cease, and you know peace and Love. Hatred and fear are buddies. They embrace each other, but their power is an illusion. Anything that is not Love does not last. Only Love is forever.

Application: Don't feel bad, at least not for long

The next time you feel out of control with any negative emotion, remind yourself that it is only a feeling created by God that is brought into effect by your free will. It is there to help you grow. Don't try to deny or stop the feeling. Acknowledge it, accept it, find its meaning, and then let it go. Listen to what you feel and allow that feeling to reveal its purpose. You may find it helpful to imagine you are outside your body watching what is happening. If you do, remember to later "become" part of the feeling again and thank God for the experience. Once you find the purpose in your emotional experience and are satisfied you understand why you feel the way you do, center yourself and allow the unwanted feeling to flow away, feeling only Love in its wake.

Myth: "Forgiveness is a loving thing to do."

Some of you are no doubt asking how this could be a myth or how believing this could cause discomfort to the person who said it. Forgiveness proposes right and wrong. Forgiveness is judgmental.

It has been written in the scriptures that God is unconditionally loving and forgiving.[2] The literal meaning of this simply cannot be true. God does not need to be forgiving or punitive, for that would suggest we make mistakes. Since the Supreme Energy did not create imperfection, there is no reason for the Universe to judge and then forgive anyone for anything. Since we are each experiencing this existence perfectly, we never need to forgive each other (or ourselves) for what we do. When we realize who we truly are, and understand the perfect process of re-discovery, we will see nothing wrong to forgive.

"Unconditional forgiveness" is merely a human construct and describes neither a duty of God nor a spiritual necessity. More helpful is a process of "reconciliation," which means accepting a different point of view and, in a spiritual way, restoring our sense of the truth. This spiritual truth is that there is no right or wrong, nothing to judge about one another, and therefore no reason to forgive what we had judged as "wrong." It is up to us to remember to reconcile with others, thereby becoming more loving and realizing our oneness with God and all of humanity.

Not needing to forgive others may be a difficult concept to accept, because forgiving has been widely thought of as sacred. In fact, forgiveness in the human sense does prevent us from dwelling in the misery of contempt and anger. By not forgiving, we hold onto "grudges" in the form of painful negative energy.[3] But these are human experiences only, and since we are temporarily human, we should make amends with

---

[2] In the old theology, God was described as avenging and judgmental. It was Jesus who attempted to put an end to this idea with his "Our Father," meaning the unconditionally loving Father of all, equally.

[3] Energy "blocks" prevent us from utilizing our full spiritual abilities. By removing these, we enhance our connection to the Divine and allow a pure flow of God's power through us for our use and benefit.

others, freeing us to move closer to Love. Reconciliation serves a similar purpose, but it allows us to realize that it is we who need to understand why we have a conflict with another person. It is we who need to understand that this conflict is in our (or the other person's) mind. And it is only we who can realize that this conflict affects our happiness in this life and that, spiritually, we needn't forgive anyone.

If you have difficulty with the word "reconciliation" and prefer to use the word "forgiveness" for now, do so. Remember, however, that forgiveness is a human invention designed to help us cope with difficulty in the physical world. Reconciliation, on the other hand, is an understanding and acceptance of the true nature of what and why things happen, transcending the physical illusion.

The first step in reconciliation is a true desire and willingness to do so. Simply going through the motions is an exercise in futility. The benefit of reconciliation is that it helps you re-member (reunite) with the Universal Spirit and your fellow human beings. Until you know in your heart the advantages of letting go of your judgments, your desire to do so will not be as great. What you think about, you keep alive. If you think negatively about the past or another person, you recreate the past, keeping that negativity and person with you in the present. Reconciliation is freedom.

To help you experience more Love through the process of reconciliation, do the following exercise.

Application: Reconciliation

There are plenty of reasons not to reconcile with someone (forgive, if you prefer, for now). It is sometimes easier not to; much more challenging is finding a way to do so. Remember, by reconciling, you help yourself. You may, of course, help the other person remove any feelings of guilt, but that is not the main objective here. By allowing yourself to understand and accept another who may have hurt you or with whom you disagree, you free yourself from the negative energy of holding a grudge and increase your capacity to feel Love.

Do whatever you can for reconciliation, but if you find it too difficult, try centering yourself and saying "What has happened in the past is over. I can reconcile with this person if I choose. I can and will do this for myself, and I will be a better, healthier, and happier person for doing so." Once you understand the concepts in this book, and how reconciliation brings you closer to Love, it will be easier.

Another method of reconciliation is to imagine yourself in the other person's position and see their actions from that perspective. Trying to understand the actions of others sometimes makes the process easier. Maybe the other person was beaten as a child and thinks verbal or physical abuse is a way of communicating. Perhaps the other person is severely depressed and says or does hurtful things out of the pain of unhappiness, believing that is all he is capable of at the moment. There has to be a reason why people act the way they do. Understanding the reason does not make the action right or wrong, and it does not necessarily make the person easier to be with or more likable. But it does help you stop feeling like a victim.

If you continue to find it difficult to reconcile with someone, try the "Love them or leave them" exercise in Lesson IX.

By choosing to reconcile, you are choosing to take back control of your life. As you do so, you are choosing to be more of your essence in your natural state — an unconditionally loving being.

As we remember we are one with the Universe, we look at the world not with pity, hatred, forgiveness, or any other emotion, but only with Love. With nothing but Love inside us, we observe the world as a beautiful place for all souls to inhabit on their spiritual journeys — a place filled with wonderful experiences and opportunities. Thank God.

Myth: "Time heals all wounds."

It is not time that heals all wounds, but Love. Time only allows us the possibility of temporarily forgetting our pains. Only Love heals these wounds. When you reconcile with Love, you release yourself from the illusory bond that the physical world imposes upon you, and only then do you create an opportunity for ultimate happiness through the healing of body, mind, and spirit.

Love is also the most important factor in healing others. If you want to best help others, first love them and then heal them through empathy and a little "tender loving care."[4] Helping others to heal is a form of prayer and creates a feeling of connectedness, which helps us know more of what Love is by our actions. When we are centered, spiritually awakened beings, we are consciously able to heal using the power and energy of God, because God is true Love, and Love heals all wounds.

---

[4] Healing is discussed in detail in Lesson VI.

Truth: Love is the answer

One of the ways[5] I receive information from my Higher Self is to "feel" it or channel it from a spiritual source. In this case, the information is not given to me but felt by me in a centered state during my meditations. Most of what I share with you here was obtained in this manner. What is it that I feel? It is Love.

After you practice the centering techniques for a while, you will know all the answers to life's challenges by how you feel about a particular choice or question when you are in a centered state.

God gave us the full range of emotions to remember what Love feels like. Once you know what Love feels like you will know what the Almighty feels like. All you will then have to do is "feel" your answers through Love, and you will be getting them from God. It is impossible to make a poor choice with this procedure for your spiritual development, because Love is the only true reality. When you feel Love in association with a particular answer, you will know it is the truth and the best answer for you.

Application: How does it feel?

Here's an example of using the "Success Tuning Technique" from the previous lesson. Practicing this technique can help adjust your mind to a level of Love, so you can make quick and accurate loving decisions.

Imagine you have to make a choice between two houses to buy, and it seems too difficult. You may feel you have no way to decide which would be best for you. After developing a basis of Love to tune into (as Dave does in the next example), a three-step process will help you make the best decision.

Step One: Center yourself using the "Basic Centering Technique" and ask your Higher Self which house to buy. Then clear your mind and allow an image or feeling to enter. If this works, act on your "intuition." Do not go on to step two or three.

Step Two: In your centered state, think of one of the houses and imagine going through your daily routine in it to see how you feel. Do the same for the second house. Don't worry if you can't accu-

---

[5] Other methods of getting information are described throughout the text and in detail in Lesson X.

rately remember the rooms — the feeling is what's important. Choose the house that feels the best, the one that feels like Love. If you are still without an answer, proceed to step three.

Step Three: Visit both houses and ask to be permitted to sit in one of the rooms by yourself with the door closed. Tell the person showing you the house that you just want to get a feel of the place. Enter a centered state in the room and clear your mind. Do the same thing in the other house, and choose which one feels like Love.

Trust and expect yourself to make the best decision in this manner, and be prepared to act on it without question. If you still aren't in touch with a feeling, either you did not reach a centered state (in which case you may need to practice more) or neither house is for you.

As God is pure Love, when you center yourself to connect with the Universe you are centered in God's Love. If you consider your feeling about something while in this state, you will be in touch with the true purpose of and use for your emotions. If you think about something in a centered state and feel uncomfortable, you are actually feeling a break in the connection to the Divine. This broken connection creates static or interference.

A broken connection during your centering practice is similar to the dissonance you hear when you play a note on the piano and sing the same note "out of tune." Any feelings of guilt, fear, anxiety, or doubt mean that you are not centered at that moment. When you are centered, there is only Love.

Therefore, when you are in a centered state and feel only Love, you can trust that feeling and allow it to help you decide. It will be the correct decision for your soul's purpose and "in tune" with the Universal Energy. If you act on your decision and accept it as already occurring (Lesson VI), you'll have created a new reality from a spiritual point of view.

Once you act on your decision, you will remember the feeling of Love you had and be "in tune" once again for a spiritual "in-the-moment" experience. Also, because you've already programmed for whatever you were thinking, the Universe will help you physically manifest what you've created mentally. Just accept the reality of your creation and sit back and wait for it to happen. If it is truly in the best interest of humanity, it will, because your thoughts are energy. When you send positive creative energy into the Universe, it is manifested in the physical world when the time is best for all involved.

Dave's memory of Love

"If the thought is right, the deed cannot be wrong."
Emmet Fox

A workshop attendee I'll call "Dave" shared an experience about feelings he had after speaking up in church. Dave, an HIV positive gay man, said he'd opened up to his church group and "bared his soul" in a situation that felt right for him. (What he said is not relevant to this example.) Afterward, he was a little nervous and not sure how it was received, but he still felt it was right at the time. He noted two quite different responses: First, one man slowly walked away and began talking with another group, which left Dave feeling uncomfortable and thinking perhaps he'd made a mistake. The second occurred as he was leaving the church. A teary-eyed older woman approached, thanked him, and said he'd touched her heart with his words. Dave told us he'd felt an unbelievable amount of Love while the woman was thanking him, but then started to feel guilty, as if he did not deserve to feel that good. He was almost in tears describing the situation.

Dave asked me a couple of questions about this experience, so during a break, I centered myself and tried to access the answers. His first was, "Why did I feel uncomfortable when the man walked away, and yet so loving when the woman approached me?" I asked how he felt when he was "baring his soul" to everyone. He said he felt peace, as if God were helping him. I told him it was possible that, in the church setting, he was in contact with his Higher Power, inspiring him to say what he did. I explained that his desire to reveal what he did was right for him (confirmed by his feeling of peace). It was not important how the man heard it, because he may not have been ready for Dave's message. But as long as the man heard Dave, the information would be part of him and his choice what he does with it. Dave did his job; the seed of Love had been planted.

The woman's response was more complicated. Dave's words were so important to her she felt it necessary to thank him. She received Dave's message through her free will and intuition, demonstrated by her choice to be present and receptive at that time. She expressed her thanks for his benefit, not hers. She could have just left but something, maybe an inner voice, told her to return Dave's Love because he needed it. When she spoke, she reminded him what it felt like to share Love. This was the "proof" Dave needed to confirm that when he acts out of Love, he helps others. The purpose of this encounter was to teach him to trust the power of Love. The next time he has the same feeling of peace and Love, he can remember this experience and the benefits of listening to the voice of Love. Love will be his guide, if he lets it work for him.

Note that I say, "if he lets it work for him," because Dave also asked why he felt guilty after feeling the woman's Love. After a brief conversation, we agreed he felt guilty for being an HIV-positive gay man who believed he didn't deserve to be happy. This limiting belief, originated in fear, might have prevented him from seeing his experience's true message. Only Love is the truth, and we have a choice what we listen to. It is only when we operate out of a faulty belief system, or are not connected to God, that we make choices that restrict our happiness.

That Dave was part of that workshop that day was also a result of his free will and intuition. It created the opportunity for him to hear what he needed to hear so he could recognize his truth. I thank him for allowing me to share his story; perhaps others will be helped by it. We are all teachers and students, and there is purpose in everything that happens, big and small. Only when we are awake do we realize this.

Once you can hear the voice of Love within, you'll recognize the feeling with confidence whenever you desire. When you act on this feeling, you help serve your individual purpose in this dimension, which is to re-discover the meaning of Love by sharing it with others.

Try the following simple exercise for expressing and sharing Love.

Application: Hug the one you love

Try to hug someone you love every day, but don't just go through the *motions*. Go through the *e-motions*. This type of emotional contact helps you feel something very pleasurable and real, if you let it. Hold the hug for a second or two longer than usual, and enjoy the experience. You may even sense what the other person is feeling. You will also be showing and sharing Love, for what good is Love if it isn't shared?

Affirmations

Repeat these affirmations silently in a centered state:
"I love each being as my own mother, father, sister, or brother."
"My journey and all others' journeys lead only to Love."
"We are co-creators with God. We can create Love."

Lesson III summary:

The answers to our questions are always available, and we can re-member them if we are unconditional loving beings. We need only re-mind ourselves that Love is our true and only nature. Once enlightened to this truth, we can experience all other emotions as opportunities to know more of Love's nature. Gaining an understanding of Love lets us re-discover ourselves every new day. By mastering this process, we re-member ourselves as pure beings giving and receiving only Love. This is the miracle of life!

When you operate from a concept of true Love, you can create miracles!

Technique #4

The Personal Paradise Technique

Purpose:

To create a special place where you can relax, heal, and maintain contact with your Higher Self. This technique is a form of passive centering; just being in this paradise heals with no conscious effort on your part. As you use your inner senses, you also develop your imaging, visualization, and other psychic abilities.

Application:

Practice the Personal Paradise Technique as often as you like. Remain in your paradise for fifteen to twenty minutes (your entire session), or just a few enjoyable minutes before continuing on to another technique.

Procedure:

Center yourself with the Basic Centering Technique. Imagine you are next to a beautiful staircase that descends to an extraordinary place. This is your personal paradise. It can be any peaceful place you choose, such as a beach or the mountains. Pick a place from your memory or make one up using your imagination. Choose your place before the exercise, or wait and see what appears.

Imagine you are on a cloud floating slowly down the staircase. Count downward at a leisurely pace, relaxing deeper as you descend. When you reach the count of one, imagine entering your personal paradise. This is a perfect place of your creation where you are completely safe.

You are alone and at peace. Bring in all the senses. Imagine the weather, and feel the sun or coolness on your body. Visualize a small brook (or the ocean) and taste the water. Note its temperature. Listen to the sounds around you — moving water, the wind through the trees, and singing birds. Breathe deeply and imagine a beautiful, relaxing aroma. Feel comfort and peace and savor the experience.

How it works:

By floating down the steps (and counting backwards) you enter a different level of your mind that leads to a deeper connection to the Universe. At this connected level, your body uses energy to heal itself as you experience your personal paradise in this centered and healthy state. By bringing in your senses, you make the experience more real to you while developing your "psychic," or inner abilities. As these inner abilities develop, your self-awareness and extraordinary potential emerge.

Additional comments:

You may want to tape record the above instructions and play them back while you create this paradise. If you have distracting thoughts, let them go. Imagine a leaf floating on the water past you and let the distracting thought float by with it. Other methods for dealing with distractions are to simply re-focus on your breathing, or concentrate on one or more inner senses you find easiest to imagine while in your paradise.

Technique #5

The Deep Relax Technique

Purpose:

To train your body and mind to experience a deep state of relaxation and connection with the Universe.

Application:

Do this technique once a day for thirty days to condition your body and mind properly. After that, practice the Deep Relax about once a week, or as often as you desire.

Procedure:

Do the Basic Centering Technique. Notice any sounds and let them go. Follow your breath for a few moments. Now breathe normally and think about the top of your head. Notice how it feels and allow it to relax. Try to create a feeling of warmth there, and release any tension or stress from this area. As the top of your head relaxes, begin to think about relaxing your forehead. Create a cool feeling surrounding your forehead by imagining it as the color blue and as smooth and cool as a piece of glass. You may even imagine a cool breeze caressing your brow. Allow this area to totally relax.

Now, imagine a beautiful white light. Creating a feeling of warmth and relaxation, breathe the light into the remaining parts of your body in this order: eyelids, mouth and jaw, neck, shoulders and upper back, upper and lower arms, elbows, hands, fingers, chest, abdomen and stomach, lower back, hips, thighs, knees, calves, ankles, tops of the feet, toes, and finally, the soles of the feet.

Once you complete this, relax and enjoy the feeling. When ready, tell yourself that when you reach the count of five, your eyes will open and you will be refreshed, relaxed, and feeling wonderful. Then count yourself out from one to five.

How it works:

When you focus on a particular part of the body, you become in tune with it. Energy is directed into the area. A feeling of coolness is created only in the forehead, to reduce headaches. In all other body parts, warmth helps relax muscles, organs, and even individual cells. White light represents energy and has a soothing and healing effect on whatever it touches. Starting from the head and working downward deepens you more than if you worked upward.

Additional comments:

If you have trouble remembering the sequence, make a tape recording of the entire procedure and play it back when you practice. After a month of practice, you will be able to reach the same level of centeredness more easily using only the Basic Centering Technique. Continue to use this on a regular basis for total physical relaxation or if you have a health problem. Use this method up to three times a day for fifteen to twenty minutes each time. However, this repetition doesn't decrease the need to practice it initially for a month. Each session should last at least fifteen minutes.

Lesson IV

The World Is An Illusion

"Our life is what our thoughts make it."

Marcus Aurelius

I magine you are just waking from a wonderful night's rest. You lie in bed for a few moments and remember a dream. You think how real it felt, and can hardly believe it was a dream. While you were sleeping, you probably didn't know you were dreaming, and thought the experience was real. This relationship between your dream state and your waking state is similar to the relationship between your waking state and your spiritual state. When you woke up you realized you were dreaming; when you wake up spiritually, you realize your entire life is a dream. When you are enlightened to this revelation, as a spiritual being, you can not only experience this physical "dream world," but realize that you *are* dreaming. You can then create any dream and life you desire.

Dreaming is a state where you experience a direct connection to the Divine.[1] To better understand the feeling of an awakened spiritual being in a physical form, use the Lucid Dreaming Technique described on page 107. This technique creates the unique experience of being "awake" and aware while dreaming. When this occurs, and you learn how to stay with your dream and not wake up until you desire, you can recre-

---

[1] You can get a similar experience by developing your skills with the techniques at the end of each lesson.

ate your dream instantly and have anything you want happen in it. At that point, you realize you are the master of your dream, losing all worry and fear. You experience a new dimension and feel a wonderful sense of power and freedom. Once you realize that you *are* a spiritual being, and that the world *is* just a dream, you can recreate your waking world without worry or fear (just as you can using the lucid dreaming technique for sleep.) You can become the master of your life and gain a conscious spiritual perspective on everything.

Application: Dream a different reality

Stay away from mind-altering drugs. If you want to alter your perceptions, do it naturally through techniques such as lucid dreaming, which creates a quite different state of consciousness and some interesting benefits.

Why the illusion?

Lesson I discusses the perfect process of the Universe that allows the re-discovery of Love. Since Love is the *only* reality in the Universe, only a *temporary illusion* can pose as Love's opposite to define it. The illusion is the physical dimension. Our Spiritual Self is the master illusionist while our physical self is the audience participant mesmerized by what we think we see.

The word "illusion" is derived from the Latin "in ludere," which means "in play." Shakespeare told us, "all the world's a stage, and all the people merely players." If you think of the world as a big play where you portray a special role, you get a more accurate idea of the nature of what you see around you. Writers write plays; you write your life. Instead of *reacting* to the world, understand that you can *act* any way you choose and write a new script at any time.

Only our Spiritual Self can accurately define the true nature of the physical world. When we remember our essence as spiritual beings in physical form, we remember world's the true nature. If you are ready to remember and transcend the physical illusion, you must first challenge your belief system and perceived impressions of yourself and the world.

Your illusory belief system

Most difficulties with your perception of the world stem from your belief system, or, more precisely, your limiting belief system. To create a new, happier life, all you need is an open mind the wisdom to challenge the belief system that currently creates your reality. Anything can be changed if you are ready. Writer John Powell asked, "What are the ifs and buts that limit my enjoyment of life?" What are yours?

Your limiting beliefs are part of an illusion holding you back from realizing your potential. Such beliefs usually come from the things you were told when young, so that you could survive on your own one day. Things such as life and death; the nature of God; making a living; marriage; right and wrong; good and bad; and much more. Without such information you would have had to reinvent the wheel.

However, some of the information you received may not have been the best for you. It was told to you by people who had it told to them by people who had it told to them, and so on. If you've ever played the game of telephone, you know that the way information is originally communicated is not necessarily how you finally receive it. The version you get is subject to the experiences, motivations, perceptions, and the moods of each person who relays the message. Most important, the information you received as a child most likely came from people who didn't know the world is an illusion and accepted what they heard and saw as "fact."

Once you are ready to make you own decision, you can take any information presented and decide if it is believable. One difficulty is that we are very impressionable when young. Information is given to us by "authorities" whom we respect, trust, and want to believe. Even if it seems wrong, we tend to accept what they say as fact because we think we have to or because everyone else does.

History provides us many examples of this type of thinking. Science is full of "facts" that are later disproved. A century ago, most people believed it was impossible to fly, but a few challenged this belief and experimented with flying machines. Once they proved the "authorities" wrong, everyone changed their beliefs about flying. At one time, people believed the stars were pinpoints of light put in the sky for decoration, that the world was flat, and that the earth was the center of the universe. Some people still believe we are only physical beings — and when we die, are gone forever.

An elephant is trained to stay in one spot by placing a very strong chain around its ankle. After repeated unsuccessful attempts to break free, the elephant accepts the belief it can't. After a while, all that's necessary is a small ankle band and the elephant won't even try to break free because it "knows" it can't. History tells the elephant so.

Put some fleas in a closed jar and they will try to escape. Once they realize they can't, they never try again, even if you remove the lid! They learn they can't escape, and believe it will always be so.

How many of us are held back with imaginary chains? How many are living in jars with imaginary lids? If we can let go of our egos for a moment, we can accept the possibility that some of the information we learned is not the truth for us and that our "reality" may not be as real as we once thought. It is never too late to change our views of the world and ourselves.

Psychologist Frances Vaughan once said, "A mind possessed by illusions is healed when it awakens to vision and Self as Spirit, eternally free." When we open ourselves to the possibilities of change, we expand our horizons to create a new vision of ourselves and our environment.

Change is difficult. We resist because we fear the unknown. If you have the courage to face this temporary fear, however, you are on your way to being fearless, forever. When you're ready for the possibility of change, try the following exercise.

Application: Challenge and change

Assess all aspects of your life. Is your world the way you want it? Do you get comfort and peace from your beliefs? Repeat to yourself, "Any reality I now see that doesn't describe what I want to see, I am changing into a more descriptive reality." You can change your ideas and, in turn, your entire life. The techniques found in this book will help you accomplish this.

The previous lessons address the illusion of imperfection. Let's challenge more illusions to help us reveal more of who we truly are.

The illusion of body

Myth: "What you see is what you get."

The easiest illusory trap to fall into is assuming what we see is all there is. Although some people report "out-of-body" experiences, the constant reminders of the physical world, and our relation to it, reinforce the belief that we exist only in three-dimensional reality. Unless you let your inner awareness acknowledge that you are of spirit in your true form, you will have a difficult time believing you are more than a physical being.

Truth: Nothing really "matters"

We are made of the same energy that surrounds and is within all living things. If you've ever seen an aura, you know that this energy exists. Auras aren't anything supernatural; they are a projection of that energy and can actually be captured on film with Kirlian photography.

To get a clearer impression of your essence, imagine yourself in a beautiful meadow. Envision energy, in the form of white light, surrounding the grass and the trees. Imagine holding your hand out and seeing this white light surrounding not only it, but your entire body, in the shape of a large oval.

Imagine some friends with this white-light energy surrounding them as well. You may even be able to see other colors in their auras. Now imagine your bodies, the trees, the grass, and everything else you believe is made of matter disappearing, leaving only their energy in the form of a beautiful white light. You can now become one light with everything and everyone and still retain your personal awareness. You will then realize you are a natural part of this light, and that it has always been connected to all things.

This exercise should give you a better picture of your essence. The only thing not present is your physical body. You are completely absorbed within Love and light. Some people call this heaven, and you do not have to die to experience it. You need only turn within and allow it to happen. As you practice, you will remember that this feeling is closer to the real you. Once you recognize you are not just a physical being, you will better understand the purposeful illusions we call our bodies and cherish the available experiences you can have with yours.

The illusion of time

Myth: "Life is short."

The physical world holds the illusion of a temporal, linear reality while the spiritual world is infinite. A linear life has a start, middle, and end, as if on a line. The only true reality is eternal and infinite because the eternal and infinite Universe created it. This true reality lasts forever; anything that dies is not real. Time is a human creation, created to measure a linear life. It measures beginnings and endings. But time does not exist in the spiritual world, because there is no beginning or ending to measure.

Humanity also created time to measure the illusion of distance. On a physical level, it takes "time" to get from one place to another. Let's examine this illusion from the three planes of awareness: body (physical), mind (mental), and spirit (spiritual). How long would it take for you to travel one mile from where you are now? Fifteen minutes? Five minutes? On the physical plane time seems real. Now, consider how long it takes you to *imagine* you are there? *No time at all.* How long does it take to imagine you are somewhere on the other side of the world? Still, no time, because time breaks down on the mental plane. Your mind knows that the physical limits of time and space do not really exist.

From a spiritual perspective, distance and time do not exist at all; everything happens all at the same time. Physically, it takes time to get from one place to another. Mentally, it takes no time to get where you want to go. And in the spiritual reality, you are already everywhere.

There is, therefore, no need to pressure yourself to do things you feel you "must" do before time runs out. Relax, and enjoy your life. You have everlasting time.

The illusion of age

Myth: "We are supposed to live to about seventy or eighty."

I have seen some clients getting on in physical years who expect their bodies to fail as they age. They are not surprised when they do and considering their attitudes, neither am I. There is much scientific and experiential evidence now to suggest that the human body has the potential to live well more than 100 years. If some people can live that long, why can't we all? Most would say the answer is genetics. This is partially true, but God did not create us to die at any particular "average" age.[2] Average life expectancies are "average" because some people are dying before, and some after that average. Most people begin to awaken to their spiritual nature in their thirties (some earlier, some

---

[2] Is it possible that we are potentially able to live each life for hundreds of years? "God only knows."

much later, and some never in this lifetime), and there is just too much more to experience and enjoy after you are spiritually awakened to die so young. Genetics may predispose us to certain diseases as a determining factor in longevity, but our attitudes and outlooks on life can greatly affect the actual number of years we have in this incarnation.

How long do you think you will live? Entertainer George Burns always expected to make it to 100, and that is just how long he lived — not 101.

Stress is the most important longevity factor. It's is all around us; physical stress in our bodies from the work we do, and environmental stressors, like pollution, from where we live and work. Emotional stress is created by misperceptions of life situations and the purpose of our emotions. Spiritual stress arises when our body, mind, and spirit are not consciously connected and we are not following our true path in this dimension.

Not all people genetically predisposed to certain diseases get them. And few, if any, actually die of "natural causes." People die of disease because their bodies can no longer counter the effects of stress that is largely created in our minds. Anything created can be recreated. If you believe that family history assures you will get cancer, you are much more likely to get it than someone with the same predisposition but unaware of family medical history. Our minds have great control over our bodies. Let's look at a couple of examples that demonstrate this.

In an "experiment," a condemned prisoner was blindfolded and told his wrists would be cut, causing him to bleed to death. Instead of cutting his wrists, however, the authorities merely applied sharp pressure at appropriate points and poured a warm liquid over them. Nevertheless, the man's belief was so strong that he actually expired as he "bled to death" in his own mind.

In another example of the mind's power, a willing participant was hypnotized and told she was going to be burned by a cigarette, which in reality was a pencil eraser. Not only did she feel the heat and pain, but her body produced an immediate blister!

Additionally, there are many cases on record where patients spontaneously healed themselves through mental effort after medical science gave up on them.

Do not underestimate your power. You are in control of what happens to you in this physical "dream world." Control over your beliefs significantly affects your life span. More important, your beliefs affect the overall quality of your life.

How old are you anyway?

Four factors help determine your actual age, and the first three are illusions. First is your chronological age — the number of years you have lived in the physical world. Even this method is not without controversy: in some Eastern cultures a child is considered to be age one at birth. Regardless, our chronological age is an illusion because it simply measures the body, and only from one perspective.

The second life-span measure is our biological age, determined by measuring physical characteristics such as blood pressure, cholesterol level, body fat, and muscle mass. We all know that a fifty-year-old can have the body of someone much younger. Likewise, we know another fifty-year-old can appear much older than others of the same age. This second way of determining age is more accurate than the first, but it is still part of the illusion of a beginning and an end.

The third measure is your emotional age, which is the most accurate measure yet. There is some truth in the cliché, "you are as old as you feel." Your thoughts determine your reality. If you feel old, you are old. If you feel young and strong, more than likely you are young and strong.

Finally, there is our spiritual age. Because the spiritual world is eternal and without time, our spiritual age is infinite. When we look past the illusion of age in the physical world, we can see that we never really age at all.

The illusion of death

Myth: "Death is the end."

The nature of, and purpose for death is discussed in detail in Lesson VII. Suffice for now to say that it is another of life's illusions, and one of the most difficult to overcome. It really doesn't matter if you have to wait until you die to discover this, but at least consider the possibility of immortality to give you more of a feeling of purpose on earth. If death were real and there was nothing more, there would be no purpose for our existence. If this were so, we would never have been created by the Universal Energy. God is eternal. God is within each of us. We are eternally one with the Universe.

The illusion of separation

Myth: "We need to find our way back to God."

It is challenging enough to realize how all humans are one. But perhaps the most deceiving illusion is that God is separate from us. We are part of God; God and we are one. Though all the world's enlightened spiritual leaders have said this, some still consider it blasphemy to compare ourselves to God. At least one person was killed about two thousand years ago for making this comparison.

Today, however, a growing number of people are remembering their connection to God and realizing that the Almighty is within. There are so many physical distractions that we must sometimes allow ourselves to first experience the Spiritual Energy through quiet meditation to feel a personal connection. After months or even years of practice, we begin to remember we are spiritual beings experiencing the physical world. When we are connected in body, mind, and spirit, we can be all loving and knowing and enjoy fully all of life's great rewards. When we realize we are one with God, we are completely conscious, and can really begin to live. As it is written in the Bible, "I and the father God are one."

The outer illusion

Myth: "Life is a game of chance."

People usually choose from two philosophies when deciding why things happen the way they do. The first is to assume that everything happens randomly. Spiritual "skeptics" often feel this way.

You may feel that luck is the reason certain people are successful. Or you may believe if someone dies prematurely he or she is unlucky. Some think life is a numbers game where some win and some lose strictly by chance.

The other view is the belief that nothing happens by chance and that everything has purpose.

Which group do you think experiences more stress? Which probably feels more detached from the rest of humanity and God. Who feels cheated when someone gains something instead of them? Which is more likely to believe the illusions of the physical and materialistic world? Whose concept seems closer to what a perfect God would have created?

You are mistaken, however, if you feel that everything happens as planned. Fate does not exist. We create all that happens, and there is a purpose for everything we create; an opportunity to experience all situations to develop ourselves as spiritual beings and an opportunity for self-discovery after the fact.

With this attitude, you need not worry about if you are doing the right thing in your life. No matter what the experience, you are more able to let it happen, and examine its purpose. You may not understand it until much later, or even in this lifetime, but there is a purpose to be realized. Lesson V helps you remember why you are here, but it is still up to you to decide which life you choose. It is your free will.

I know someone who feels that everything happens randomly and that he is the victim of bad luck. Actually, he is quite a nice person; he makes me laugh and I enjoy his company. But he lives day to day, with little faith in himself or the power of the Universe. He has no aspirations except to make money. He acts as if humanity has no purpose for being, except to live and, eventually, die. I asked him, "What if you're wrong?" He replied, "Could be, but I guess I'll find out when I die."

His logic may be correct, but do you think he's really happy? I assure you he's not. He is not taking advantage of all the wonderful gifts and experiences of an awakened being. His life is still his choice. I told him what I've experienced and he listened. It's now up to him. Maybe one day he will remember who he is and experience true happiness in this life. Either way, we'll meet again in another dimension and have a good laugh.

Myth: "I am a victim of a cruel world."

Carl Jung once joked that we should kick a blind man whenever we see one. He asks, "Why should we be kinder than God?"

Because the world is an illusion, your impression of what you see and feel is all that matters. If you believe you are a victim of your circumstances who was dealt a bad hand by the Lord, it's understandable if you have a negative outlook on life. Some people go through so much pain as children that it is a wonder they grow up with a positive outlook on anything. Nevertheless, some do, and they don't just survive. Their resiliency and determination prevent them from remaining victims of the past. They somehow find the power within to reconcile their feelings about those who hurt them. At the very least, they don't blame themselves for the actions of others. Then there are those who continue to suffer. They view the world as a cruel place and see themselves as powerless victims. This illusion of a cruel world is reinforced by all the negative information on the news about tragedy and unfairness.

You do have a choice. And always had, but didn't realize it. Understand there is spiritual perfection in all that happens, and that there can be peace within when you've become enlightened to the illusory nature of the physical world. If you feel you've suffered greatly, or have a very negative attitude, it may take a lot of time, hard work, and practice to feel the presence and perfection of God within you. But others have been through the same, or worse, and succeeded. There is nothing anyone has done that you can't. You may have all the time in eternity but why not try now? You are here anyway; might as well make your life work.

If you bear emotional scars or are suffering, who better than you to realize how good it would feel to suffer no longer. Once again we see the perfect process of the Universe at work: we go through pain so we can know peace by comparison. Continue to center yourself until you can feel that the illusions of emotional and physical pain are for no other purpose than to know Love.

Reporting the illusion

If you believe the world is cruel, do not blame the news. The media do a wonderful job of providing what majority wants to watch, read, and hear. They reflect our illusory views of the world. When the attitude of the masses changes to Love, the news will feature more loving stories. It is up to us to choose what we watch and read. We decide how we want to view the world.

When Princess Diana died, many blamed the photographers who chased her for pictures. Yet these same people rely on the paparazzi to show them what is happening in the lives of the famous. These paparazzi only reflect the world's priorities. If we don't like something, we must first change our own beliefs. The natural effect of that change is the end to the things we no longer need. When there is no demand for grief, there will be no supply.

Like everything, Princess Diana's physical death had a special purpose. It reminds us we are sometimes too involved in the lives of others, using their lives to distract us from our own. As centered human beings, we no longer need live our lives through the reported exploits of celebrities. Instead, our experiences can fuse us as equals. The need for the paparazzi will disappear only when we find our true nature as one with the Universe and when we unconditionally love and respect ourselves and others. Perhaps then their roles will be redefined to help us share Love more easily.

What is our reality?

If the physical world is an illusion, does that mean we are? Are we a soul? Are we spirit?

The spirit

The spirit is God, Love, and the one energy force of which we are all a part. God needed a form that could enter the human dimension and feel all the emotions of each human experience. Only then could the Almighty Spirit feel by experience what Love is not in the physical illusion in order to know Love in the spiritual reality. The form created by the spirit was the soul.

The soul

There is only one spirit, but there are many souls. The soul is like a finger where the spirit is the hand. If the Universal Intelligence created only one soul, there would only be one experience for the Almighty. More souls mean more experiences and opportunities for re-discovery. The soul is a form of the spirit that can enter the body. Since the soul is part of the spirit, and the spirit is God, we are the manifestations of God in the physical dimension. The soul chooses to whom it is going to be born so it can best help itself, and all other souls, on the journey of re-discovery.

After entering the body, the soul is neutral. It does not force its will on the mind or body (see below). To affect the perfect process, the Spiritual Intelligence has chosen to give the human mind free will so the soul can "feel" all possible experiences. The soul feels each experience and corresponding emotion and decides if it is Love.

Each soul is on its own journey. Although it would develop more easily if the mind and body followed its chosen path, the soul understands the nature of eternity and is satisfied to experience all that the physical world has to offer in any given lifetime. There is no rush to fulfill (or penalty for not fulfilling) the soul's purpose in a lifetime. Time does not exist in the spiritual world.

The mind

The Universal Mind is God, which is One. The Universal Mind is of the spiritual world and contains all the information of all minds. This is similar to what Jung referred to as the "collective unconscious." The individual human mind is a projection of the Universal Mind and a part of God. It has all the creative ability of the Universe, which makes each person a co-creator with God. The human mind has free will to create any physical world experience it desires.

Whatever the human mind creates, however, is an illusion, because it will not last. Everything in the physical world, including the body, is an illusion. Only that which remains after the body is gone is real. This is why only Love is real. All experiences that the mind creates lead to Love as part of the perfect process of re-discovery. The individual mind can, however, create total happiness in this lifetime if awakened to its reality.

Through "transformational amnesia," the human mind forgets it is a part of God and that there is more to life than that experienced by the physical senses. This amnesia is a necessary part of the perfect process, since all the experiences must seem real (as we revealed in Lesson II). Knowing who we truly are when born would make it impossible for the soul and the spirit to experience the true nature of what Love is not.

The individual mind can operate on its own by using the same creative ability that created it. If awakened and centered, the individual mind consciously receives guidance from the Universal Mind, which always points it toward the most purposeful direction.

The individual mind has information continually available to it from the spiritual world in intuition, dreams, "chance" meetings, and opportunities created by the all-knowing Universal Mind. It's up to the human mind to choose to see this information.

The individual mind exists in and around the body, but it can consciously transcend the body and connect with the Universal Mind if in a centered state. We naturally make this connection while dreaming, but with the help of centering we can be "re-minded" any time we wish.

The brain

The brain is part of the physical world and therefore part of the illusion. The brain does not think by itself; that is the function of the mind. The mind is the computer programmer and the brain is the hardware, or processing unit. It carries out the thoughts of the mind as orders and does exactly what it is told to do. The brain programs the body.

The body

The body is a temporary physical creation; it's the printout of the mind and brain. It's purpose is to allow a more "real" experience for the soul through physical sensation.

Transcending the illusion

To gain a new spiritual insight into the "authenticity" of what you think you see, first realize that you create your reality by your beliefs. If you change them, your world will change. A massive shift of beliefs changes the entire world. This is happening now as humankind, as a whole, becomes more conscious to spiritual reality.

Because we are the co-creators with God, it helps to understand the process of creation. A myth we all heard in our youth describes a hazard in the physical world. It begins, "Sticks and stones may break my bones, but..."

Myth: "names [words] can never harm me."

Nothing can be created without a thought. If you think about making a table, for example, the first step is the original creative thought, not the materials or the blueprint. Thoughts create our physical world, and actions (including words) are the catalysts that make thoughts physical reality.

As the programmer, your mind has the option of what type of information will eventually be printed out. The printer, or body, is just a machine that produces exactly what it is told to print. If you *think* you have a bad back, you are sending that image to your body and to the Universe to produce and maintain for you. Neither the Universe nor your body knows if you really want to experience this condition.

The Universe cannot choose what is best for you. Your mind has that power and the free will to choose your experiences. The Universe knows there are no good or bad experiences, so it gives you what you program. Because the Universe and body respond to requests literally,[3] be careful how you ask for something. If you think negative thoughts, they are like magnets in attracting our fears to us.

I have heard many stories with the same theme:

There was a man whose favorite expressions were, "I just can't see your point," "I can't take it anymore," and "She's a pain in my ass!" Today, he wears glasses and has an ulcer and hemorrhoids. Sounds funny, but it isn't. This person created his physical maladies and didn't even know it. He also has the power to reverse or at least halt this process but doesn't know that, either. Instead, he perpetuates his illusion of poor health.

Watch what you say. You would be amazed at how negative your thoughts and words can be. Whenever you catch yourself saying or thinking something negative, stop, and restate it in a positive way. For example, instead of "I don't like my boss," say, "I could like my boss a lot more." This thought is sent out to the Universe in a positive form. Instead of "I feel sick," at least say, "I could feel better," or preferably, "I am better." Not only are you being positive, but you're communicating to your body and the Universe that you "could feel better," so you will. With the proper positive thoughts you can create a new you if you really want to.

The first step is to monitor your thoughts and words.

Application: Learn a new language

Not a foreign language, but a new language full of positive thoughts and helpful words. Always watch what you say. When you catch yourself saying something negative, erase the thought as you would use the delete button on a computer and replace it with something more positive and helpful.

---

[3] Even in dreams the information you receive is literal, although coded with symbolism. For you to benefit from this information, you must interpret the correct meaning to what is there.

Affirmations

Repeat these affirmations silently in a centered state:
"I am the creator of my world and my reality."
"When I see and feel Love, I see and feel the truth."
"Life is what I create it to be."

Lesson IV summary:

When you remember that the physical world is a purposeful illusion and embrace the power of your creative ability, you can direct your life experience. You may also choose how these experiences affect you. Then you can stop being a victim and take control of everything that happens to you and recognize things for what they truly are.

If you are not happy with yourself or not the person you feel you can be, change who you are by changing your beliefs, thoughts, and words. When you create a new reality for yourself and the world around you, you create a new you. When you are one in body, mind, and spirit, you'll understand that the physical world is just an illusion for re-discovery and for our pleasure. You will then be one with all of humanity and one with God. In fact, you already are. Remember?

Love is the only true reality — all else is illusion.

Technique #6

The Dream Log Technique

Purpose:

To remember dreams for the purpose of insight and enlightenment and to benefit from the Lucid Dreaming Technique on page 107.

Application:

Do this every night until you can remember your dreams without the need to write them down. Use the Dream Log Technique to allow your dreams to assist your journey of re-discovery.

Procedure:

Keep a pen and paper by your bed. When you wake up during the night or in the morning, record anything you remember about your dreams. Do this until you can remember a few dreams in detail. Then center yourself with the Basic Centering Technique, think about a dream, and clear your mind to reveal its meaning.

How it works:

By writing down your dreams as soon as possible, you prevent their loss. Everyone dreams, although some people have a hard time remembering them. This technique helps develop good dream recall, which is a must if you desire to understand these messages from your Higher Power.

Centering yourself and clearing your mind allows awareness of your intuition, which tells you the dreams meaning.

Additional comments:

Keep a dream journal on a regular basis as a sort of diary. Dreams help you know where you are in your life. When first attempting this technique, don't try to interpret a dream's meaning unless you are in a centered state. Once you've learned to decipher your dreams, you can use them as guides and even ask for answers to appear in them before you sleep.

Technique #7

The Lucid Dreaming Technique

Purpose:

To develop the ability to "wake up" or become conscious in your dreams and know you are dreaming. Use this technique for healing yourself and others, for fun and exploration, and for getting information from your Higher Self.

Application:

Developing this skill results in very rewarding experiences. Practice the Lucid Dreaming Technique until you can have a lucid dream on command. This may take a lot of practice, but it will be well worth it.

Procedure:

During the day, think about lucid dreaming. Repeat as often as you think of it and during your centering exercises, "Tonight I will have a lucid dream." Repeat this in a session before you sleep. It may help to put a rubber band around your wrist as a visual reminder to repeat the saying. Throughout the day, think about lucid dreaming and the type of lucid dream you want to have (see the different types, below). You may also try meditating on the center of your throat (where the sixth, or throat, chakra is located), which Tibetan tradition says enhances the process of lucid dreaming. You should have a lucid dream within the first few nights. If you have trouble with this method, wake two hours earlier than normal, center yourself, repeat the saying, and go back to sleep. You are then more likely to have a lucid dream.

How it works:

Lucid dreaming is a state of mind where the unconscious and conscious meet. It provides awareness and direct contact with the spiritual reality. By planting and repeating the suggestions to have a lucid dream, you give your unconscious the message to produce one. This works the same way as affirmations. As you gain more control over the process, you learn to program such dreams at will.

Additional comments:

There are four types of lucid dreams. The first is for fun and adventure. In this dream you can fly, go through walls, live out your sexual fantasies safely, or do anything else you desire.

The second type is for physical and spiritual healing. You can imagine yourself, or anyone, in their present condition, and wave a "magic healing wand." Seeing them healed and happy programs it to occur in the physical world. Because this state connects you to the Spiritual Energy, you may find this application of the Lucid Dreaming Technique extremely effective.

The third type of lucid dream is for receiving information. You can ask questions of any person in your dream. This person is a part of your Higher Self, so the answers come from the Universal Intelligence. (An example is presented in Lesson X.)

The fourth type of lucid dream is for interpretation. Simply allow whatever is happening to continue to happen and choose to understand it. Do not alter the dream, just make every effort to be an observer, trying only to grasp the meaning in its message.

Lesson V

We Are Each Here For A Special Reason

"Whatever path a man travels, it is my path. Wherever he goes, it leads to me."

Unknown

Though we are all one energy force, one mind, and One Spirit, each soul incarnated into a specific form on earth for a unique purpose. We are here to experience different situations and similar situations differently, and to share these experiences with the Universe, our total consciousness. There are many different journeys to share. This is why there is more than one soul experiencing this world.

Your journey is now and exists at this moment, whether you realize it or not. It will be more enjoyable if you consciously pursue your spiritual purpose to bring the world to Love. You do this by expressing Love in whatever you do, and most easily express it when doing what you do best. Consciously following your spiritual purpose brings you ultimate joy, balance, peace, freedom, and happiness.

You have seen them. He is the conductor exuding power and poise as his orchestra performs a beautiful medley. She is the lawyer who fights for her client's life as if it were her own child on trial. She is the waitress who serves customers with as much enthusiasm and caring as her personal friends. And he is the gas station attendant who still cleans your windshield even when his co-workers won't. Who are these people? They are spiritual beings who breathe life into their work. They are people who express themselves in what they do, and not simply for financial reward. They do it because they couldn't do their job any other way. They are living their soul's purpose and consciously doing what they do with Love, and they are happier than most.

Have you ever felt something missing in your life? If so, this could be the reason: The soul has a twofold purpose in each lifetime: (1) the *universal* purpose to re-discover itself as Love, and (2) an *individual* purpose to experience a specific role it can do better or differently than any other soul in a given lifetime. The latter enables the soul to help itself and other souls more easily re-discover Love. In other words, your individual purpose is the best way to promote the universal purpose.

Spiritual stress

Myth: "Life is like a pressure-cooker."

Many clients who solicit my services seek assistance for reducing stress in their pressure-filled lives. They are usually unaware that they're feeling "spiritual stress" from being disconnected from their individual purpose. By living with this, or any, excess stress, they remain unaware of themselves as spiritual beings and their wonderful journey of re-discovery. Too much stress prevents you from becoming conscious to your truth. Thus, it is vital to your happiness to reduce your stress level, so you can re-discover your Spiritual Self with fewer distractions.

Stress exists only in *this* dimension, not in the spiritual world. Spiritual stress occurs when you are not in touch with your Godly self or following your *individual* purpose the way you are God-gifted to be. The difference between conventional and spiritual stress is that, in the latter, you feel confused and usually can't pinpoint the cause of your anxiety. This leaves you feeling melancholy or with the uncomfortable impression you aren't living up to your potential. You may begin to resent your life, the people around you, and even God.

The best way to overcome any type of excess stress is with a regular program of relaxation and meditation. The centering techniques in this book can help you greatly. Relax, follow your soul's purpose, and consciously live each moment of your life as a spiritual being. Peace comes from within, and is there whenever you desire to feel it.

There are no "ideal" jobs. Not every person should be a healer or a teacher. We need conductors, lawyers, waitresses, and gas station attendants. Each person lives his or her purpose by performing his or her job in a spiritually loving way, which reaps the many rewards of a purposeful and relatively stress-free life.

Application: Relax to find your purpose

All the applications in this lesson are to help you find and live your individual purpose. However, most of us should first reduce our overall stress levels by practicing one of the techniques for stress reduction and general relaxation within this book. Practice at least twice a day until you feel less tension in your everyday life. Stress prevents you from focusing energy on your true purpose and remembering who you really are.

If you feel you aren't pursuing your purpose in your job,[1] do the exercises in this lesson before quitting. You may be surprised to discover you are in the right line of work after all, but just not doing it the right way for you. This realization may enlighten and empower you to enjoy your job and life more fully.

Truth: We are special

Each of us can do something totally unique. The challenge is to discover your spiritual "niche" on earth, so you can realize your potential for happiness. If you live untrue to this niche, your energy will be unaligned with the Universal Energy, and you are likely to feel something missing in your life. You'll experience a feeling of dissonance, which can lead to disease.

Let us suppose, for example, that in this life you can best serve the journey of Love by expressing yourself as a salesperson. But because of your free will, you did not choose that line of work. This can cause "dis-ease" in the form of unhappiness or even physical illness. Disease is a sign you aren't following a connected life, body, mind, and spirit. Clients who discovered this and how it was best for them to work, achieved more gratification in their lives. Some actually healed their physical conditions just by making certain changes in how they perceived their

---

[1] You can, of course, live and follow your purpose even if you aren't "employed."

work. By understanding and living their individual purpose, they filled the void created by a disconnection to the Divine and removed the feeling that something was "missing."

Application: Hit the lottery and know your purpose

One of the surest ways to know if you are living your purpose is to imagine winning the lottery and having all the money you'll ever need. If you'd choose to continue doing what you do, it is surely your purpose. The rewards of living your soul's purpose go far beyond money. If you think you'd retire, you may just be burned out. If you *do* hit the lottery, take a vacation and then do what you do with Love, instead of just going through the motions. You never need to retire from Love. You can always serve your purpose and enjoy what you are doing and how you are doing it for a lifetime.

When you are connected to your spiritual purpose, your life becomes easier and more satisfying and rewarding. Why? Because you are no longer operating as an isolated individual out of tune with the Universe. Instead, you are working *with* the Universe, consciously connected to the Universal Mind and utilizing the vast potential of the energy around you. When you find your true purpose, the Universe has no choice but to help you by providing information and energy.

Truth: Our purpose is to move toward Love

This book asks questions such as, "why wait?" or "why live an entire lifetime with unhappiness?" But is also says that everything is part of the perfect process and there is nothing to worry about. This may seem a contradiction, so permit me to clarify. There is no penalty for not fulfilling your soul's purpose in this lifetime. There is no rush to do so. In fact, you chose to live in the illusion until ready to awaken. You had to; this was purposeful for the process of re-discovery. However, once you begin to awaken, you are ready to take a giant step toward spiritual awareness to realize your purpose for existing. Illusions begin to fade, and you live a more loving, fulfilling life. When we develop spiritually, we move toward an ultimate and eternal loving paradise. Why wait?

Let's look at another example, returning to the metaphor of *Thermostats*, *Thermometers*, and *Sleepers*. For this example, assume that warmth is more desirable than cold.

Sleepers live in the cold parts of the world and don't know that warmer climates exist. Cold is their only reality.

Thermometers live in seasonal climates, enjoying the changes in weather. Because these individuals know both cold and warmth, they can re-discover and appreciate the nature of warmth by comparison.

Thermostats once lived in cold or changing climates and moved to warmer ones. They chose to remove themselves from the cold, because they don't need it to define, understand, and appreciate warmth.

The *Sleepers* forget why they are here and dwell only in the physical aspect of their lives. They aren't aware of other ways to live. The *Thermometers* are searching for their purpose, while the *Thermostats* have found the reason their souls chose this particular form. When awakened, everyone can live his or her purpose. Once you find yours, you'll achieve a level of happiness never before experienced. Only then will you know who you really are. It is your spiritual journey to move toward the warmth of Love and enlightenment. By consciously living your soul's purpose, you'll follow the guidance of the Universal Energy, which makes you "warmer" and happier.

Myth: "Other people have better lives."

Many of my clients arrive wishing they had other people's lives. They regret who they are and compare how they are living to a preconceived notion of what life should be. Because life is an illusion, however, there is no truth to anything in this physical dimension. Each is on his or her own journey, and no individual should be envious of another. Each of us has his or her *own* special purpose. What is best for another may not be in *your* soul's best interest. The awareness of your life purpose is very personal and one that needs to be discovered from within.

We are the powerful creators of our lives. We have the gift to choose how we live. No one need live in envy of another, or as a victim. You are the creator of your life and the co-creator of the world. No one can be better at being you than you.

Myth: "Our purpose is to learn life's lessons."

We are all-knowing spiritual beings, so there are no lessons to be learned.[2] As part of the Universal Intelligence, we already inherently

---

[2] "The Awakening," explains why the chapters in this book are entitled lessons.

know all there is to know. If you know what hot is and put your hand on a stove, you are only experiencing and *remembering* it. We can be "taught" to remember that which we have forgotten we already know. We are here to experience the physical form, and have the ability to remember we are spiritual beings. Think of this book as a "refresher course," with information, tools, suggestions, and techniques to help you remember what you already inherently know. Life is its own refresher course. You are here to remember who you really are. Relax, and let it happen.

Inherently, we know we are Love. Once we remember this we understand our desire to enjoy and share the Love we already have. Your individual spiritual purpose is also something you inherently know. When you remember why you are here, you'll experience a very familiar feeling that seems just right for you. This feeling is an enrapturing sensation of Love.

Myth: "My life is a waste."

Our individual purpose is part of the universal purpose, which is to re-discover Love. Discover and do what you do best to serve your individual purpose, but also remember that everything you do serves the universal purpose, no matter how you live. Your life is never "wasted." The benefits to living consciously and pursuing your innate God-given talents are greater self-awareness and happiness. But no matter how you choose to live, accept who you are now — a wonderful creation — and remember that life is a journey not a goal.

To fulfill their individual purposes, some people may not actually have to ever "do" anything. They can just "be." Within the perfect process there are many unusual and mysterious ways that help us remember Love. Some souls choose to be born with severe physical challenges. They are spiritually advanced souls who decided before birth to help by allowing others to love, help, and care for them. Some souls chose to assist the perfect process later in life, inspiring others by overcoming seemingly impossible physical challenges, and other souls through personal tragedy, as in the Christopher Reeve example. Everything has purpose.

Truth: Teach Love by being Love

No matter how anyone helps another they always help themselves. It is very satisfying to help others, especially those suffering the disconnection of not knowing who they truly are. This feeling of satisfaction is Love's reward. Sometimes people accept your help while other times they don't. Don't get frustrated. Just give the message of Love by expressing and being Love.

At times, it may seem your efforts to help others are worthless, or that they aren't getting the message. If this is the case with someone you care about, use the techniques and applications in this book to love, pray, and help them at the spiritual level. Then accept that you've done your best. People are on their own journeys, and it is not up to you to "save" them. They too, are the perfect creation living the perfect process. Simply share Love and information with them, and trust the Universal Intelligence.

Before I understood this, I often got frustrated with people I cared about who wouldn't take my advice. I now realize I was being judgmental. My heart was in the right place but I underestimated them and forgot about the perfect process. I eventually discovered my individual purpose was to "re-mind" people, not to *convince* them of anything. My role was to empower others with information they could verify and accept or reject as they chose when ready to do so. When I remembered to trust the process, I was less frustrated. Here is one example:

A client I will refer to as Jeff came to see me filled with anger. He was angry at himself for his life choices, which included smoking, taking drugs, and working at a job he hated. He was angry at the world for enabling this and angry with God for letting him down by not answering his prayers. We spent a few sessions discussing the messages set forth in this book.

Jeff was highly skeptical, but he *did* listen. Just as he began to feel better, he quit therapy. He believed he was going to be let down eventually and had no choice but to continue to numb himself with drugs to avoid his pain and the feeling he would always be a "failure."

A few weeks later I received a letter from him. He said he'd quit drugs and smoking and was enjoying his job more. He thanked me for helping him see things differently and assured there was no need to worry about him. By then, I had learned to trust the process and never doubted that things would work out for Jeff.

Truth: Teaching Love is purposeful

We are all teachers and students. Teaching and learning (or remembering) are the same, just as giving and receiving. Because we are all the same spiritual being, the process of teaching and learning has great purpose. It is the sharing process of Love at its best. Without this process, there would be no growth.

A great way to understand something and express yourself is to teach others. I discover the most about myself when I counsel, present seminars, and write.

When you teach (or help others remember) from a centered position, you are in harmony with the Universe. It generates energy you are most able to tune in to (Lesson I) and keeps you motivated to stay on course. When you live your purpose by doing what you do with Love, you co-create perfection with the power of the Universe. Because it is truly pure, it makes everything seem easy. Your life will be more simple and fluid, and you will be much happier and more satisfied. The results of your efforts will be a reward not only to you, but all those touched with your effort. As the Universe helps you, you find you are rewarded with everything necessary to help you continue.

To realize your spiritual journey, understand you are very special to the world. You can become more consciously aware of this journey today, regardless of who you thought you were yesterday.

Truth: Love will guide you to your purpose

Let's try an experiment. Read one line at a time of the following scenario, then close your eyes and try to see and feel what is described. Imagine you are walking down the sidewalk at your local supermarket when you spot an elderly woman in need of help. You walk over to consider her situation and notice her shopping cart wheel is stuck in a crack. She asks for your help. Imagine reaching down and removing the wheel from the crack and then purposely and maliciously turning the shopping cart over, spilling her groceries to the ground. When she asks why, instead of answering you knock her to the ground as well. She begins to cry and you laugh in her face.

How does this make you feel? Do your emotions tell you it is your essence to hurt another? If this scene feels comfortable, please make an appointment with a therapist, now! I hope this doesn't describe who you are. *If you don't feel Love, you don't feel the truth.*

Now let's replay this scene. This time, you help the woman get the wheel out of the crack then look at her lovingly. She smiles, blows you a kiss, and says, "I'm happy I met you. The world would be a better place if there were more people like you around." Does this feeling tell you more about who you really are? Does it define who you want to be? Finding your purpose can be as simple as following the path of Love. It always takes you where you really want to go.

Application: Who are you?

Ask yourself, "who am I?" Is it who you want to be? Are you surrounded by people you admire and respect who feel the same way about you? If not, you're probably not being who you want to be, doing what you spiritually desire, or performing what you do in a spiritually loving manner. Change anything you feel is not Love, and your entire world will change. If you are a musician, but always felt in your heart you wanted to be an electrician, decide in a centered state if being a musician "feels" like the best way you can express Love. If not, change your job.

If you constantly get upset at people, try showing them Love instead. Make the changes your heart tells you to make and you'll be on your way to realizing a more purposeful, enjoyable life.

Signs from within

If you are centered, the Universe helps you find your purpose by giving you information. It can come in the form of a dream, through intuition, a "coincidental" phone call, a "chance" meeting, or by an overwhelming feeling of Love that lets you know you are on the right path. If you are more conscious, you will be more able to recognize these signs. Once you begin living your purpose as a spiritually loving being, you will remain that way for the rest of your life.

At that point, you can simply ask, "If I were God, what would I do in this situation," and feel the answer. It doesn't matter what happened yesterday, because if you did, said, or even thought things that did not describe who you feel you want to be, you can change today. In this moment you can follow your heart and become an unconditionally loving and accepting person. Is there something you're doing that feels uncomfortable? This could be a sign you aren't acting out of Love and are not in harmony with your Spiritual Self. What you are doing may be very beneficial for someone else to do, but it doesn't take advantage of *your* individual talents.

When you center yourself, you are more likely to be receptive to your emotions and the information around you. Centering helps you discover or *feel* what is best for you. If you merely go through the motions, you may find yourself doing something from habit that neither describes the real you nor realizes your true talents.

I often used to go to casinos because I loved the action and thrill of winning. Even losing didn't bother me that much as long as I felt the excitement and had a chance to win. Everyone else seemed to be enjoying themselves, too, and the atmosphere was always filled with emotion.

At my wedding, my brother gave a rather humorous speech about my frequent trips to the Atlantic City casinos. I had a sudden feeling of discomfort. What he said was not insulting in the least, but I felt I'd given him (and maybe others) the impression that gambling was an important part of my life. Although it rarely bothered me what others thought, it *did* bother me that the story didn't describe who I really was or the person I wanted people to know. I was not using my individual gifts to the best of my ability to help people re-discover Love.

After this incident, I continued to gamble though less frequently. I found I didn't enjoy myself as much. I'd look at others and feel I didn't belong. It wasn't a matter of feeling judgmental; I just felt out of place. This was an important sign, and I realized there was something wrong with *why* I went to the casinos. While centered, I discovered I enjoyed gambling because my life was not as purposeful as it could be. I used the casinos as a substitute, or diversion, in an attempt to feel more excitement in my life. They mimicked the "high" I wanted to feel, a high I subsequently learned I could produce on my own.

From this experience I knew that I was not fully on purpose in my life. So I shifted gears to discover what could create the missing excitement. That's how the process of self-discovery works. Our emotions are powerful tools that provide valuable information when we listen. One point needs to be made here: if you are pursuing your spiritual purpose, there's no reason you can't enjoy gambling (or anything else). But you'll enjoy these experiences as a conscious spiritual being who does not *need* to do anything but simply enjoy what life has to offer. The difference is whether you are trying to replace a missing feeling or enjoying something for experiential purposes only. Are you doing what you do (hence, being who you are today) because you *need* to or because you *want* to? Do you control your life or does the illusion control you?

Signs are always available if we are awakened. It doesn't matter how you find your purpose. It's only important that you do discover that which allows you to express yourself fully. Practice all the applications in this lesson, and you will get your answers.

Application: Help from your spirit guide

Many times it may seem easier to find your purpose by asking questions of a "person" instead of the Universe. If so, practice the Spirit Guide Realization Technique (described ion page 193) and ask your guide your purpose. You may get the answer. If so, trust it, because it's from God.

Myth: "You must search [outside yourself] for your meaning."

A common problem is putting too much faith in others and not enough in yourself. There's nothing wrong with getting assistance from others, but each of us is on our own personal journey. Other's can only help you discover the best path by giving you the techniques to do so and by sharing information and their experiences. No one except you can define your individual purpose.

Truth: There is only now

Enlightenment, or the meaning of our life, takes time to discover. It's part of our wonderful journey that has no goal or end. The journey is all there is and "the now" we all live and always will. By consciously living in the now, you can cease worrying about the past or future and enjoy your life now.

Part of enlightenment is knowing there are no goals except to re-discover yourself as Love. You are doing that now as you read this. Your soul may want many lifetimes to discover or clarify your true essence. Don't worry; you will eventually know and be one with all. In fact, you already are — remember? Don't put too much pressure on yourself to do any specific thing you feel you "must." You are part of a perfect process and when ready, you'll have all you desire. For now, love your life.

Application: Live in the now

The past no longer exists and the future will never get here. The now is all there is. No doubt you've sometime said you'll start something tomorrow. Tomorrow is always tomorrow. Accept things as they are today as part of the perfect process. Repeat the affirmation, "Live for now, Love for now, there is only now."

If you don't like who you were in the past, let it go. The present is all there is, and you can be the real loving person you truly are — today.

Goals in life

Myth: "My purpose is to accomplish my goals."

Goals are not a problem. They become a problem only when they take us out of the present and force us to focus only on the future. We all have goals and a desire to attain them. They are strong motivating forces that help us survive. But goals are created for the physical world and are part of it. Therefore, they are part of the illusion. If you desire a new goal, live every single moment of your life as Love now.

There are many physical goals (improving health, making more money, finding a mate, etc.) but they are not of the spiritual reality. Your Spiritual Self wants nothing except to re-discover who you are. Although your physical goals are important to you, accomplishing them is not even what you really want.

Everyone who pursues physical goals wants the feeling of success and security they believe these goals will bring. The challenge is to balance your goals so they don't control or engulf your life. Take the time to enjoy your accomplishments. Live in the now and allow yourself to relax and pursue your journey of healing for body, mind, and spirit.

Once you remember you are a spiritual being, you can have fun with goals. Set up physical challenges to help you experience the joys of attaining these goals and the disappointment of falling short. Of course, once you remember you are a spiritual being, the disappointments won't create the same emotional response or last as long because you know they are not real.

If you create your world in the best way for your individual energy to express itself, your spiritual goals and physical goals will be in line and you'll have a very easy life. Your energy will "resonate" better. For example, if your spiritual purpose was to be a physical healer in this incarnation, and your earthy goal is to become a doctor, accomplishing it will give you great satisfaction.

From the Universe, you'll get the emotional reward of a sense of fulfillment, oneness, and a feeling of ease. You'll also get financial rewards, which allow you to enjoy life without the worry of paying bills. This in turn allows you to give more of yourself to others, who can then help others.

You may be an interior decorator whose purpose is to create a pleasant decor for others, including the doctor, which produces a friendlier atmosphere for her patients. All jobs are needed, and each is as important as the next. Some people make music while others listen; each relies on the other. When we operate on purpose, we more effectively help each other remember who they really are, and remember ourselves in the process.

I often wondered why so many who do their soul's work struggle financially, while others not following their purpose get rich. The answer that came in a centered state was that there's no fooling your Spiritual Self. True happiness cannot be bought. If you equate happiness with money, then that is your reality. But your happiness may be only temporary because money, like all illusions, can disappear. When you're serving your soul's purpose, you are rewarded with the feeling of Love, which is more valuable than money. Love is real and lasts throughout eternity.

Myth: "Your goal is to be successful."

As with some of these myths, it all depends on how you look at it. What is your definition of success? Unfortunately, our society has the tendency to think of the word as synonymous with "financially successful." This places a lot of pressure on us to make money to get the recognition from others we think we need. We do not need others' recognition if we are completely centered. As you become more conscious of your Spiritual Self, you may find the need for money diminishes.

Most spiritual masters in our history did not have great financial wealth but were more content than those who did. You can have money if you really want it (Lesson VI), and it can certainly help you to enjoy pleasurable physical experiences. But if your goal is simply to make money, you will likely end up trying to do only that all your life. In the process, you may actually miss out on what money can help you enjoy.

Success

What does success look like? Can you paint a picture of it? If so, would everyone else agree it was a picture of success? Or would it only be your interpretation of it? Success is subjective and finds its true meaning only when you are fulfilling your soul's purpose. Because each soul has its own purpose, everyone's success is different. Until you are living your purpose consciously, it's likely your idea of success will change constantly.

The physical world offers much for our physical senses: relationships, houses, careers, cars, appearance, and money, to name a few. Achieving any one of these could be viewed as success if you desire it enough. What distinguishes material gains from spiritual success is that physical successes always leave us wanting more. Spiritual success is the realization that you already have it all and don't need anything to feel successful.

Your desire to experience life is a reality, not a goal. You're already living that reality perfectly. Feeling truly successful is consciously experiencing life as a spiritual being in a physical form, which is all you really need do. Fulfilling your individual purpose is actually just being and living as Love.

Realizing you don't need to achieve anything outside yourself is a difficult concept to accept in the physical world. If it's easier to feel you must accomplish something to feel successful, concentrate on the goals created in a centered state. These give you the greatest sense of fulfillment. With practice, you'll eventually see you lack nothing, and don't need to achieve goals to feel successful.

The purpose of religion

Because of the subject matter of this text, it may be helpful to clarify the purpose for religion. This will help you decide if a specific religious affiliation works best for you, and if so, to help you enjoy its most beneficial aspects.

"The kingdom of heaven is within." - Christianity

"He who knows himself, knows the Lord." - Islamic tradition

"Look within, thou art the Buddha." - Buddhism

"God dwells within you as you." - Siddha Yoga

"Atman and Brahman are one." - Hinduism

"I in Thee, and Thou in Me." - Jewish tradition (Moses)

Lesson 5: We Are Each Here For A Special Reason

Religions vary, but the underlying message couldn't be clearer. The purpose of all religion is to help you remember yourself as true Love, and to know that the Almighty is not far away but within. Religion is a path to understanding that we are united with God.

This spiritual truth is the core belief of all the world's great spiritual masters, past and present. When centered, you feel this truth. You are a master in the making.

Religion is not the only path to God, there are many. If you choose to make a specific religious affiliation yours, enjoy it. But don't think you life's purpose is to become religious. The ritualistic nature of religion is employed to evoke spiritual awareness. Don't get too caught up in literal messages. They are easy to misinterpret. A vow of celibacy can be viewed by some as a message that sex is bad, but its actual purpose is to transcend temptations of the body by concentrating on the spiritual nature of shared Love. It's a message to not restrict our view of sex to merely a physically satisfying experience with one person. But to allow a sexual (non-physical) freedom and sensuality with all people.

If you find religion helps you remember you're a spiritual being, then it is serving its purpose in your life. It's a matter of personal choice.

If you don't fully understand your religion's message, this conclusion might upset you, possibly because an "authority" has threatened you'll be punished if you don't follow what he or she says.[3] Perhaps you were "taught" to be hateful or resentful of other faiths and think yours is the only true religion preferred by the Almighty. Maybe you were taught to defend your religion as the only true path to the Lord's word.

More people are killed in the name of God than by any disease. Do you think this was God's intention? You have a choice, and the ability to overcome the seeming differences of those around you to see and feel the underlying unity of Love.

Spiritually enlightened individuals see harmony between the world's great religions; others see only differences. Wouldn't it be wonderful if congregations of all faiths practiced their religion by actually listening to the words of their founding inspirational figures? The pursuit of Love is at the core of all true religion.

If you are religious and love your faith, look deeply into it to find

---

[3] Roman Emperor Constantine did just this. He used the name of God to convert people to his beliefs and eliminate other religious sects. His impetus was to control social order, not to allow religion to lead people to re-discovery

true Love. This will help you find heaven within and live your purpose. If you read or hear anything that separates humans from God or humans from each other, question your interpretation. And question those who use hatred and fear to control others, they are serving their physical egos, not Love. Religion and objects of worship are there to evoke a state of spiritual connectedness. They are means, not ends.

Myth: "My life is in God's hands."

You have a choice how you live and experience this life. Take charge of your experiences and enjoy yourself at this moment.

If you are waiting for God to choose your path, you'll have a long wait. But if you choose life *with* the Universe and live as Love, you'll affect your purpose each moment. You are the co-creator of your life and everything you see, so you can create the life you want. Time does not concern the Universe; the concept doesn't exist as we understand it. Accordingly, there's no reason for the Almighty to force something to happen for you. The Universal Intelligence understands it's all happening now through the perfect process.

It is up to us to remember why we are here, but don't feel pressure that you must, or must not, do something. There are no musts. You can choose to live as you wish; and only you can decide if your life is the way you want it to be. If you feel something is missing, only you can create a lifestyle that fills the void. Don't leave it up to others by sitting back and hoping. Use the sixteen techniques in the book to connect with God to create a life of Love.

You may know someone whose favorite expression is, "If it's meant to be, then it's meant to be." This person seems to be filled with faith in something outside of themselves. If you are centered and in line with your purpose, the Universe helps you create your life. Then what happens seems like it's meant to be. Life will seem easy and effortless, as if on automatic pilot. You'll live each moment "in-the-moment" and enjoy a meaningful life. Most important, you'll understand that you created each moment. By becoming a more loving person, you make a conscious effort to align with your purpose. The alternative is feeling little control over what and when things happens to you and little control over your happiness.

Application: Dreaming your purpose

If you think you know your purpose but aren't living it, use the Lucid Dreaming Technique to help you make the transition. Imagine being the new you in your dreams to see how you like it; there's no risk! If you want to know what it feels like to be a construction worker, use your dreams and sense the emotions that go along with it. With time, you'll be able to rely on these emotions and experiences for guidance. If you want to be a politician, be one in your dreams. Decide if it works for you, without running a campaign or even leaving your bed!

Affirmations

Repeat these affirmations silently in a centered state:
"My purpose is to uniquely help the world to re-discover Love."
"Although our paths differ, all journeys lead to Love."
"Everything I do, I do with Love."

Lesson V summary:

Living your purpose means doing what you do best; doing what you do with Love. By doing so you consciously continue God's work by creating, re-creating, and expressing Love in each moment of your life. You re-create yourself every day. Today, create who you really want to be, living your true purpose. Only then will you realize wholeness in body, mind, and spirit.

Find your purpose, find your life, find yourself.

Relax, You're Already Perfect

Technique #8

The Theatre Technique

Purpose:

To use mental imagery and visualization to create a new "reality" by effecting a change in the physical world. This includes creating happiness, health, wisdom, and wealth or realizing any desired goal or life experience.

Application:

Practice as often as necessary to program change or action.

Procedure:

The first time you use this technique, center yourself and imagine yourself in your personal paradise. Note where the sun rises in your paradise. Then, make a quarter-turn right and picture a theatre in the distance. Now imagine walking, floating, or flying there. (After the first time you do this, you can enter your already-created theatre without going through your personal paradise.) As you enter, there's a large stage concealed by a closed curtain straight ahead. Go down the aisle, sit in the center seat of the front row, and look up at the closed curtain. You see a big number "10" on the curtain, which begins to count down. Concentrate on the numbers, imagining them changing colors and shapes. When you reach the count of one, watch the curtain open to reveal an empty, and well-lit stage. Create an image of the situation or person (this person could be you) you want to change. Allow this image to walk into the scene from the wing on your left and stop there to face you. Visualize a white ball of light a foot above the image, full of energy and spinning slowly and powerfully. As the light spins and gains energy, imagine it flattening and spreading out wide long enough to cover the entire image. Now imagine the still-spinning, completely flat light moving slowly downward, touching the top of the image and passing through. Imagine whatever it touches changing to the way you want it to be. Stop anywhere that needs special attention and keep the light there as long as you want before moving downward. When the light reaches the stage floor, imagine the entire person or object is exactly as you wish. See the person or object happy and moving. This "new" image is now a created fact.

Once you watch this new image for a couple of minutes (you can have a conversation with it, if you like), imagine leaving your seat and moving toward the right part of the stage. Climb the stage stairs and face the object or person, even if the person is a "new" you. Move toward it while the image moves toward you. Meet in the center of the stage by the count of five and touch, smile, laugh, and dance, if you wish. If the other image is you, imagine combining into one. Feel yourself as the "new" person and keep that feeling.

Now imagine the stage disappears and a new scene of your own invention replaces it; any scene you desire. Experience this scene with the "new" object, person, or self, just as you want, using all your senses to make it more real.

After completing this programming, let go and accept that it will be manifested. It will if it's best for all involved.

How it works:

This is an incredibly powerful technique. Sitting in the center of the first row, you naturally look up at the curtain. Turning your eyes upward triggers Alpha waves that help you get more deeply centered. Watching the count descend from ten to one, deepens your level of mind. As you watch your "project" enter the left of the stage and get healed by the light, you create (in the future[4]) a healed image of your desire. When you enter the scene from the right of the stage (the past) and move toward the new image, you bring the past and future together

---

[4] According to Jose Silva the founder of Silva Mind control, the left is the spiritual future.

into a new present. Once this happens, you tell the Universe this is the new reality that has already occurred. By bringing in a new scene and using your senses, you reinforce this new reality.

Additional comments:

Once you create the desired result, you don't need to repeat this exercise until a change occurs. Instead, reinforce the new reality by visualizing a scene using the result of your creation. Reinforcing this image while in your personal paradise is most effective. While centered (but also in your waking state) think about the newly created image and reinforce it. If you effect a change that's not exactly what you want, decide if it's best for all involved. If so, stop visualizing the original result you wanted. If you feel it's not the way it should be, see only the finished result you desire. What's best for all involved will eventually manifest itself.

If you like, imagine the image (person or thing) as already changed as it appears on the left part of the stage. This is a more passive approach preferred by some. But still imagine the image coming from the left wing (from your center seat perspective).

If you're not sure what you should be doing with your life, the Theatre Technique can help.

Imagine you're living your purpose. Don't think about what you're doing with your life, simply allow yourself to feel the wonderful, positive emotions of being "spiritually successful."

Envision standing on the stage and hearing someone knock on a door. Open the door and visualize an old friend asking what's new. Tell him or her you are finally doing what you do best, what your soul intended you to do. When your friend asks what that is, say the first thing that comes into your mind. This is most likely the right thing for you. If nothing comes to mind, just smile and tell your friend that it's a surprise. Either way, enjoy the loving feeling of success you have envisioned.

If you can recognize the loving feeling of spiritual success, but don't know what you can actually do with your life to make this a physical reality, you can, in a centered state, think about a few possibilities. Imagine doing one of those things. When you feel the same feeling of success connected with any of your ideas, it will be the thing that will feel like Love to you — the most purposeful thing for you.

You may be thinking about a new career or you may be surprised to discover you're already doing what you do best for yourself and humanity. If you find you're already living your purpose but aren't happy, you may be doing it with the wrong attitude. You are now beginning to understand who you are, and can now do what you do, with Love.

Technique #9

The Sensory Enhancing Technique

Purpose:

To practice your development of mental imagery and the ability to use your inner senses. This technique can also be practiced to improve your effectiveness with the Theatre Technique.

Application:

Practice this if you have difficulty conjuring images with the Theatre Technique. Practice it until you can use the Theatre Technique to your satisfaction. Once this happens, you needn't do this exercise again to help you in the theatre. But you can use it anytime you want to enhance your imaginative abilities.

Procedure:

Go through the same procedure as the Theatre Technique until you open the curtain. Now imagine pieces of food, preferably fruit, appearing one at a time, floating and spinning slowly above center stage. Imagine one floating toward you and notice how it appears to get bigger as it approaches. Try to sense how the food feels. Imagine its odor and bring it to your mouth, thinking about how it sounds and tastes as you bite into it. Now envision the food floating back to the center of the stage, spinning slowly, hovering, and disappearing. Repeat this with many different types of food. After you're satisfied with how this works for you, visualize other people in the scene, eating some of the food while you watch. Or think about sharing a delightful snack with them.

How it works:

By imagining familiar things, you develop your visualization and imagery abilities. By imagining seeing, feeling, hearing, smelling, and tasting food, you are developing your "psychic" senses. Bringing in people after you are comfortable with the process, develops your imagination and visualization skills.

Additional comments:

You have always had the ability to use your creative abilities and were probably very good at using them when you were young. You may have forgotten how to use your imagination and merely need to practice. Your creative abilities, perhaps dormant, will reawaken and develop easily, when you have an open mind.

Lesson VI

Live For Abundance

"The secret of success is constancy to purpose."
Benjamin Disraeli

Spiritual abundance embraces the concept that that everyone can have everything they truly desire. Once you accept there is enough for everyone, you stop worrying about competition and allow yourself to experience everything you ever dreamed. No spiritual rules prohibit what you desire. You can live abundantly if you use the power of the Universe to create prosperity.

You can create abundance in your life *now*: a life full of ultimate happiness, better health, financial wealth, and the wisdom of King Solomon. You can also have a lot more fun while developing and experiencing the physical world. Unparalleled abundance is the reward of living life as a spiritually awakened being and following your purpose to make the world a more loving place.

What do you need?

"There is enough for everyone's need, but not for everyone's greed."

Mahatma Gandhi

Myth: "I will be happy when..."

What do you think would truly make you happy? Let's suppose one of your answers would be to make more money. If you were given a million dollars but told that you couldn't spend it, money would do you no good. If you were allowed to buy a house that no one could live in, you would find the house worthless, too. So what do you really want? If you don't know, you'll greedily pursue material things, thinking they will satisfy your needs.

You already have everything you really need and just have to realize that within.

What you truly desire is abundantly available and not limited to the resources of the physical world. Experiencing Love is all you *really* want. Money, treasures, even good health and better relationships are all things you *think* you need. But they are all part of the illusion. They may be important in this dimension, but when you are completely awakened with Love, you realize you need nothing else.

This doesn't mean you can't work at a great job, have better health, or enjoy life's material rewards. These things are for you to enjoy and experience *only* while you are here. Once you're an awakened spiritual being, you're free to consciously experience all of life's physical rewards as an *addition* to your life, instead of believing you need anything for wholeness and happiness. You may say, "Yes, but love doesn't pay the bills." Survival is important of course, but merely surviving is not our purpose here. We're here to enjoy this illusion and re-discover who we are.

Three steps to abundance

> *"Therefore I say unto you, what things soever ye desire, when ye pray, believe that ye receive them, and ye shall have them."*
>
> *Mark 11:24*

If you are ready, you can get anything in this fantasy world in only three steps.

Step 1: Know what you want.

This means the feeling *behind* what an object or person will help you to experience, not the object or person. Lesson IV discusses how the

Universe responds literally to your thoughts, so be as specific as possible. For example, don't wish for a better marriage when you really want to share peace and Love with another soul. Don't think you want better health when you really want more energy and the ability to experience life. Health is a means, not an end. Think carefully about what you really want, so when you program for it, you'll create a clearer picture in your mind (and Universe) so it can more easily be manifested.

Step 2: Believe you can get what you want.

You can't have something if you don't believe you are capable of having it or deserving of it. It's not enough to merely desire something; you must believe you are capable of owning it. If you're 5'9" and believe no one your height could dunk a basketball, you never will.[1] (But no one told that to 5'7" professional-basketball-player Spud Webb.)

Application: You deserve abundance

If you think you don't deserve something, challenge this belief. Where did this idea come from? Is it a reality? Center yourself, and ask for an answer. You will find God created you to experience prosperity and abundance in all things. There is nothing you don't deserve.

It is said that anything you can conceive and believe, you can have. This is almost the case, but if you want help from the Universal Energy, there's one more step.

Step 3: Accept that you already have what you desire.

Once you accept that you've already received what you created in your mind, the process is complete. If you sprain your wrist playing tennis, see it healed using the Theatre Technique. By creating in your mind that your injury is *already* healed, that image will be manifested in the physical world, and you will be back on the tennis courts much sooner. If you want to find a loving partner, center yourself and create an image of *already* enjoying your life with the person you desire. (It is not necessary to know who it is or to imagine a face.) If and when you are ready, the Universe will unite you!

---

[1] If it were truly your soul's desire to dunk a basketball, you would probably have chosen a taller body!

Don't ask!

Thought is energy. This form of energy is processed by your creative mind and printed out as your reality. If you're centered, you co-create your print-out with the power of the Universal Energy. Your thought will be much stronger, resulting in the creation of what you desire sooner.

"You can never get what you want, but you can love all you have, and you can have everything."

Sounds like a riddle, doesn't it? By understanding and applying its secret, you unlock your potential for abundance? You can never get anything you want, ask for, or pray for, because your body and the Universe knows only how to give you more of what you already have.[2] Nothing more, nothing less. Getting confusing? Hang in there.

When you *ask* for something, what message are you giving the Universe? The Universe hears, *"I do **not** have what I want!"* If you tell the Universe you want more money, you're really saying, "I want more money because I don't have enough." Why else would you ask for it? If you had enough, you wouldn't need to ask for more. When you ask or pray for more money, you are programming the Universe to create (or maintain) your *not having enough money!*[3] By telling the Universe that you already have what you desire, (*i.e.*, enough money), you program *that* thought. "I have enough money" is exactly what will be printed out for you.

The print-out you see could be a "coincidental" financial gain, or maybe an advantageous business opportunity. Perhaps you will "out of nowhere" gain a feeling of peace and security with what you already have.

Truth: A picture is worth (at least) a thousand words

The only way to create anything is to tell the Universe to bring your future desire into the present. How do you do this? Create a picture, or blueprint, of the *result* you want to be printed out for you. Instead of

---

[2] The Universe operates only in the present because the future doesn't exist in the spiritual reality.

[3] The next myth explains how God does not interpret your desires or answer your prayers. God created the perfect process, which doesn't need adjustments. You are the creator of your life and can use your energy to create whatever you truly desire.

asking for your disease to be removed, center yourself and create a picture (the Universal language) in your mind without the disease, feeling the way you want to feel. That picture will eventually be printed out if it's for your soul's (and all others) best purpose. Accept your mental picture as fact. This may seem as if you are lying to yourself, but that shouldn't concern you; be concerned only with creating what you want. This is the best way to do so using the full power of the Universal Energy.

Want a better job? Imagine yourself already having it; the Universe will help you like your job better or find a new one. The Universe has no choice in this, as you are part of it.

If you follow the program in this book, you'll have everything you truly want. If what you think you want doesn't appear, it's possible that you may first need to practice the techniques longer to get them to work. These are skills everyone can master, but may take time developing, just as any other skills. If you master the techniques in this book but are still not receiving what you *think* you want — think again. You are part of the Universe, connected to everything and everyone, living the perfect process. It is possible you already have what is best for you and humanity. If so, you already have what you *truly* want, whether you are conscious of this or not.

Prayer

Myth: "God answers prayers."

I know that at least some of you are now saying, "This time he's going too far." Relax for a moment and remember that God has already answered your prayers with your creation.

God will not answer your prayers, because God doesn't need to. The Almighty knows you have everything already. It is futile to ask for help correcting something the Universe knows is already perfect. Instead, consider praying and thanking God for giving *you* the power to answer your own prayers. Thank God for the ability you have to create and experience happiness, better health, great wisdom, and more wealth. Praying in this manner, actually tells the Universe you accept the power God-given within you. And it will be so.

Consider adding this to anything you program for: "Thy will *is* being done,[4] and I'm happy and loving of any result because it will be the most purposeful for humanity." It always was and always will be. You are God's co-creator and the maker of your world. Anything you desire and pray for will be answered when you realize *you* have the power to create anything you want to experience.

It's not necessary to be humble before God; constantly asking or begging for help in what you perceive is a powerless existence. You are part of the Universe and have God's power within you. If you place your life in someone else's hands (including God's), you overlook the perfection of your creation and place the onus of your wishes outside yourself. This is no different from waiting for a miracle to "happen" to you. You were created to recreate. Spiritually awakened people see miracles every day, and know *they* created them.

The famous psychic Edgar Cayce said, "Prayer is inviting the spirit of God to flow through us." Mr. Cayce realized that we best create our lives and our realities by expanding our level of awareness and connecting with the Universal Energy, and allowing that power to flow through us for our benefit.

There's no limit to what you can create and receive. You can even pray (program) for past events to change in the "reality" of today.[5] The spiritual reality is not limited by the concept of time. For now, understand that the only limits you have are the ones you *create* for yourself.

Let's now look at happiness, health, wisdom and wealth, and the self-limiting and self-defeating myths that prevent you from realizing you *can* (and do) have what you desire.

Abundant Happiness

> *"To deny ourselves pleasure is to deny pleasure to God as well."*
>
> *Rabbi Eleazar HaKappar Berebi*

What's stopping you from being completely happy? A client who felt she'd given everything and received nothing in return told me the

---

[4] The expression, "Thy will *be* done" suggests fate and proposes a future result. The modified expression, "Thy will *is being* done," makes the affirmative statement that we were already perfectly created, and that each event we create is purposeful in moving us toward Love.

[5] If this interests you, read Larry Dossey's *Healing Words*.

following myth. As a result, she always felt disappointed by others.

Myth: "People are too selfish."

No one does anything for another without there being something in it for themself. This may sound selfish and unreasonable, but it's not. When you do something for another, you may or may not be aware of the benefits to you. There is always a "selfish" reason, one just for you. You may disagree and say, "I help because I want to and ask for nothing in return." You have, in fact, stated what's in it for you. You help because it makes you feel *good*. To be more accurate, you help because it makes you feel *God*. The Almighty gave us the emotions to recognize when something feels good. Those positive feelings are a very strong reward. You can think of this as selfish if you choose, but it's natural to be selfish in this respect.

If you feel guilty about experiencing true happiness, remember that the more happiness you have in your life, the more you can share with others. Taking care of *you* first is not selfish; it's necessary for survival. And helping yourself helps all others because we are all One.

There's a type of selfish that's not beneficial, which occurs when you deprive *yourself*. By not allowing yourself true happiness, you deprive yourself of the experience of knowing shared happiness. You're not giving, so you're not getting anything in return.

Myth: "If we serve ourselves, we are not serving God."

If you understand the fallacy of the previous myth, you can see how serving yourself is not only the right thing to do, but the holy thing to do. If you're spiritually awakened, you know you are a part of God and every living thing. *You and all your brothers and sisters are the same spiritual entity.* Because we are united as One, and the One Spirit shares each experience, everything you do for yourself pleasurable for your soul is pleasurable to the Universal Spirit. When you strive for happiness in abundance, you are serving everything and everyone as well as God.

If you don't understand this concept of spiritual abundance, you'll never allow yourself to receive what you truly desire and deserve. You'll struggle, searching the material world for something that can only be obtained within.

"All I want is to be happy"

I worked with a very depressed client in her early twenties we'll call Debbie.

Debbie felt that she should have been married by the age of twenty. It didn't matter when friends told her she had plenty of time, or that she was still very young. In her "reality" — stemming from a difficult childhood where she didn't gain the important sense of security — she felt she had to be married to be happy. Debbie had a boyfriend she tremendously pressured to marry. When the relationship ended, she attempted suicide to alleviate her desperation. They eventually married, but she remained unhappy. Then she felt a strong desire to have a child. It became an obsession, and she again put pressure on her husband. They may or may not have been ready for a child. She longed only to find a missing sense of security.

After giving birth, Debbie now hoped a new home would bring the peace of mind she sought. After the house, another child. No matter what she attained, she remained unhappy. Debbie may or may not have been aware that these possessions would not help her, but she knew of no other way to find peace and happiness "within herself." Ironically, this was the only place she didn't look. After some time in therapy and practice in centering, she was finally able to fill her emotional void by finding Love and security within.

Myth: "We must sacrifice to reach heaven."

Some people don't allow themselves happiness because they were trained to believe that doing without, or sacrificing, is holy. It's not God's intention that anyone sacrifice anything for any reason. If you choose to do without in your life, and many religious people do, it should be because it is your choice about how you want to live. It should not be because you feel you must.

God created the world, including all the beautiful things in it. Do you think a perfect Creator would tempt us to enjoy the pleasures around us and then punish us for doing so? God does not play games. Jesus said, "I AM come that they may have life, and that they might have it more abundantly." Don't worry, live abundance. If the Universal Intelligence didn't want us to do and have the things that make us feel good, we wouldn't have been given the emotions which dispose us toward doing pleasurable things. God is Love. If you truly love something and are centered, enjoy it. In a centered state, you feel the truth.

Myth: "If it feels good, I must be doing something wrong."

If you feel guilty for living life in abundance, it is probably because you don't yet understand God's purpose for creating the physical body, and the physical experiences available. Some go so far in accepting the "if it feels good, it must be wrong" myth, they create psychosomatic illnesses to compensate for the guilt for having and enjoying something "sinful." We deserve all the happiness the material world can help us experience. Do you feel God would be deprived of anything God desired? Of course not, why should you? The choice is yours.

This book does not suggest to automatically conform to the "if it feels *good* do it" philosophy. Connect with the Universe through a centered state and then do it, *if it feels God.*

Application: Are you really happy?

Define true happiness for you. Note if your answer is based on material or spiritual desires and you will know your path. Material desire is fine. But this exercise may help you understand that energy spent on pursuing something material only delays true happiness. True happiness is inner peace.

Sports and hobbies

Myth: "Sports are for jocks."

Participating in sporting events or enjoyable hobbies helps keep your physical self alive, alert, and happy. The physical dimension brings many great experiences, all assisting in the re-discovery of your Spiritual Self. If you do something physical as a spiritually awakened being, you can more fully enjoy it and do it better.

Before my mental training, I was an average athlete. My visualization and imagery training helped me become one of the best athletes in my sport in the country.

When people begin centering, they usually have a goal in mind. They want something from it like relaxation, or a spiritual connection. Or maybe self-improvement in sports, hobbies, or other recreational activities. It doesn't matter why anyone intends to get in touch with their

Spiritual Self, just that they do. The benefits from being connected to the Universe are realized no matter what you think you seek. When you're connected, all your abilities improve, including clarity in thinking, intuition, better health, and athletic competency.[6]

You can improve whatever you want. The concept of spiritual abundance places no limits on you. You can have whatever you desire, because you already have it. The ability to be a better athlete was always in me; I just needed to tap into the Universal Energy that was around and within me, so I could take advantage of all I could be.

Application: Do whatever you do better

Once you've accepted the spiritual reality that you can happily enjoy yourself and have as much fun as you want, this exercise will help you do everything better. For this example, I'll use the sport of golf.

Center yourself and imagine a time when you played an incredible round of golf or even when you hit just one shot perfectly. If you can't bring back a "real" memory, use your imagination and create an image to serve as your memory. Bring back the feeling you experienced during your success so you can refer to whenever you need it.

You can now "tune into" this feeling (as in the "Success Tuning Technique" from Lesson II) and bring back as many of the sights, sounds and other internal senses you can. Use your natural imaginative ability to re-create that scene, feeling as if you are there again. All you need to do before performing again is close your eyes, take a deep breath, and tune into that memory. Once you have re-created this feeling of success, imagine what you are about to do will bring you the same result. Make sure you picture the final result — the sound of the ball entering the cup, not the putt. Then clear your mind and relax. Put yourself on auto-pilot and just let it happen. Be present in the moment: ready, energetic, relaxed, and confident, all at the same time. With a little practice using this exercise, you will improve your physical ability tremendously.[7]

For a wonderfully energizing experience before a sporting event, prac-

---

[6] Those of you who remember Arthur Ashe's "upset" victory over Jimmy Conners at Wimbledon in 1975 may recall he meditated during each crossover. He was truly centered on center court!

[7] Jack Nicklaus, perhaps the most famous golfer of all time, said he would never take a single swing without first creating in his mind a clear picture of what he wanted to happen.

tice the Chakra Balancing Technique described at the end of this lesson.

Sex

Myth: "Sex is only for procreation."

Nothing makes most people feel quite so guilty as recreational sex. At one time or another, most of us were told that the sole purpose of sex was procreation. Nonetheless, we eventually experimented with sex and found it felt very good. So good, we continued doing it in spite of the message that abstinence was "holy," except for creating children. Adolescents ask, "Do I listen to what I was told, or to what my body is telling me?" Most listened to their physical sensations and decided sex was something they were going to experience anyway, but not talk about with parents or other role models. It would remain a secret, almost like consorting with the devil. If you are female, you were possibly given the additional message, "good girls don't do that." A girl who liked sex was "loose," maybe even "sinful." I can only imagine how difficult it must be to live as a teenage woman.

Little wonder that adolescence is a time of emotional confusion that causes eating and other adjustment disorders. If you're a male who "fooled around" as a teen, you may have been considered "cool" but still doing something "wrong." This created a conflict that may have caused identity problems and a disconnection between body, mind, and spirit.

God *created* sex and the feelings that go along with it. Those feelings of ecstasy are as close to feeling Heaven as we possibly can in our present form. The guilt we feel about recreational sex stems from our limiting belief systems. The Universal Intelligence didn't need to create something as wonderful and beautiful as sex, only to punish us for enjoying it. Once you realize this, you'll be ready to take the next step in exploring your sexuality, making it a spiritual as well as physical experience.

Sex as an enjoyable spiritual experience is something that can enhance our connection to God. Let go of your ego, fear, guilt, anxiety, and desire to control or dominate another physically. Enjoy the incredible experience of re-discovery through sexuality by living and loving in-the-moment.

Does this suggest that we should have sex whenever, wherever, and with whomever we please? That's up to you. It's part of your free will. But most of us live in a society as a whole that still frowns on pre- and extra-marital affairs, homosexuality, and certain kinds of sexual acts. Whatever we decide, there are consequences to our actions; a cause-and-effect scenario that could land us in physical trouble. *Not* spiritual trouble. There is a difference between the two. Physical trouble includes disease, marital problems, unwanted pregnancies, jail, etc.

These are real problems for as long as we dwell on this planet. After this life, it does not matter to God (or to you) what you've done, as all situations would have been experientially beneficial. But while you are here you are wise to make the best decisions for everyone involved in your sexual life. It may be wonderful to experience sex with many people to better enjoy the sharing of Love. But until the world changes its attitude about sexual relationships, we'll still have the problems manifested by those beliefs.

Application: Sex in the moment

Repeat the above application, "Do whatever you do better," and replace golfing with sex. Before engaging in a sexual activity, try centering yourself and remembering a time when you enjoyed a beautifully romantic experience. Recreate all the wonderful feelings you felt. When you are ready, open your eyes and bring those feelings with you in the new experience you are about to have. Let go of that memory and become totally present with who you are with.

It's also a good idea to have your partner do the same, and for both of you to be "tuned in" to the Universe and each other. This will bring more spirituality into your sex life, making it more satisfying and enjoyable.

Abundant Health

The medical profession has finally accepted that stress can cause or exacerbate disease. It has even given the specialty a name – psychoneuroimmunology. What may still not be understood is that there can also be dis-ease when the individual mind and physical self are disconnected from the Universal Mind. Without a conscious connection to the Divine, the body, mind, and spirit cannot function as a unit. If this occurs, an individual may make choices not in line with her soul's purpose. This "disconnection" can create "dis-ease," which is the manifestation of this uncomfortable state.

Everything in life has purpose — disease is no different. It usually tells you that you're not living a lifestyle suited to you. Whatever has no purpose ceases to exist: your body is no exception.

Healing, more accurately described as "ultimate functionality," takes place when Love is felt and happiness achieved. Healing occurs when there is a recognition of unity and balance with the whole — the awareness of oneness with the Universe. Jung said healing is the result of the pursuit of a "greater and stronger life urge." There is no stronger life urge than Love. As you move toward Love, you move toward healing.

Myth: "God causes diseases if we do something wrong."

God created humanity, humanity creates disease. We do this through the power of free will using our God-like creative abilities. If you do something unhealthy it can cause a great deal of stress. This stress can precipitate the body's breakdown of its natural defense system, causing sickness or disease.

While this cause-and-effect may be obvious, it may not be apparent that by feeling you are doing something wrong, you might unconsciously feel you don't deserve to be happy or healthy. You may be sending a message to your body and the Universe that you should be unhappy or ill. That's the message which gets a response and a print-out. On a larger scale, consider the possibility that if enough minds are thinking negative thoughts about something, a disease can be created that reflects that energy.

Consider the AIDS epidemic, for example. AIDS is transmitted in many ways, but most people think of it as a sexually transmitted disease predominantly affecting gay males. Further, many believe homosexuality to be a sin, something "against the will of God." I even heard a well-known, influential speaker tell an audience that God created men and women to be with each other to procreate the species. Homosexuality went against God's wishes. He went on to intimate that AIDS was the punishment for violating God's wishes.

Whether you believe this or not is not the issue (although remember that God has no need to judge or punish). What's important to understand is that if enough people think this way, including some gay men themselves, it should be obvious how a disease such as AIDS could be created. When the attitude of the masses changes, so does the manifestation of the massive power of collective minds.

Do not underestimate our power. Free will allows us to create any experience we desire in our lives. It doesn't matter to God how we choose to live in the illusion of the physical world. It is all part of the perfect process. But if we want to enjoy *this* life, we must use our creative abilities to create an enjoyable experience.

As humanity's recent shift in consciousness towards spiritual awareness continues, more of us will move toward spiritual healing. As we move in this direction, the need for disease will gradually cease.

Myth: "My condition is all my fault."

I've consistently heard this myth perpetuated by people who only partially understand the process of creation. We do create every aspect of our human experience, but I wouldn't be a good therapist if I told people they are the cause of all their problems.

The answer to this dilemma came to me in two parts while centered. Humankind created all the diseases with which it has been inflicted. It is part of our free will. Once again, we observe the perfect process of the Universe working its magic, as *dis-ease* leads to *ease*, helping us know Love.

I was satisfied with this from a spiritual point of view, but it didn't help me from a clinical perspective. Then I received the second part of the answer — "*We all do the best we can at every given moment.*" I'd heard this before, but hadn't understood it until I needed the information. Given where we are at any moment, operating with all the knowledge and experiences we've had in the physical world, we exist with a current temporary "reality." Our response to any current situation in our life is a *natural* response, given our current belief system about that reality. Nothing is ever our fault, nor is there anything to actually be blamed for, because we always do only the very best we can every given moment.

Once you're aware your belief system can cause or perpetuate disease, and realize that you have the power to change these beliefs, it becomes your responsibility to re-create your life today to be healed. Ignorance is not stupidity; it is simply not knowing yet. Now you know. If you want to be healthier, create it. Healing is the difference between doing all you thought you *could* and remembering how to do all you really *can.*

Most people are not concerned with the how and why of illness, only how to remedy it. There are three reasons for the perpetuation of illness. If you are ill, understanding which situation applies will help relieve your suffering. In most cases, by putting your creative power to work, you'll be able to alleviate your symptoms and quite possibly the entire condition. By doing so, you will be more able to enjoy this life.

1) Illness can maintain itself through the law of cause-and-effect.

On the physical plane of awareness, if we don't take care of our bodies, we are subject to environmental toxins, the effects of stress, and the mental and physical results of a sedentary life. On the physical plane, disease seems to be something that happens *to* us, and out of our control. This illusion can create a feeling of victimization.

In most cases, you are the cause and your condition is the effect. If you don't want your car to start, don't turn the key. Cause is simply how you choose to think and live, and effect is the result.

If cause-and-effect is the only reason for your ill health, you'll be able to heal your physical condition by understanding and applying the techniques in this book.

2) Illness will persist if we are caught in the illusion.

On the mental plane, our mind's (unconscious) desire to experience all that the physical world has to offer to satiate the soul, causes it to create many seemingly undesirable situations, including illness. Your condition, in this case, would be for a purpose.

However, due to the powerful nature of the illusory world, it's possible we aren't aware when this purpose is achieved. We may live in the "reality" of our disease and accept it as fact. In this case we are actually programming for our illness to maintain itself, and receiving exactly what we programmed.

A man built a raft to cross a river. He was so pleased with the raft's usefulness, he decided to carry it with him on land, too. He didn't understand the raft was no longer needed, and created a burden from what was once a blessing. Understand there is a purpose for everything, including illness. See that purpose and let it go when it's no longer needed. The river you are now crossing is the unknown. As a spiritual being, your awakening allows you to leave your "rafts" behind and begin a wonderful life, living each moment with Love.

On the mental plane, feelings of victimization fade when we understand we have the power to control at least a part of what happens to us. How much control we have is related to how much awareness we have of our power.

If your current condition is maintained by being caught in the illusory "reality" of your illness, you'll again be able to heal yourself when you master your "new" skills.

3) The purpose of our illness reaches beyond personal experience.

On the spiritual plane of awareness there is no disease or suffering. Everything that happens has purpose, and all of life's situations move us to Love.

Some souls chose to be here to inspire others. Minds in line with this purpose may have a "negative" physical condition. People learn a great deal vicariously about Love through their perceptions of the pain and mental anguish that others experience. We remember more of what Love is not, and painfully, but purposefully, we move closer to Love.

Since it's possible that the purpose for your condition is serving the needs of the whole, be patient and have faith in yourself and God. Your attempts to heal the symptoms may not help at this time since the purpose for your condition has not yet been effected. But you need not suffer the anxiety of not understanding. Realize that you are consciously or unconsciously in control of your condition and that your pain or discomfort does not control you.

Author and speaker Joan Borysenko remarked, "Healing is a remembrance of our own true essence." If you want to be healed physically, understand that when you ask for "perfect health," this may include pain and disease. Illness may be the perfect thing for your soul or the souls around you. When someone is said to be healed, that may not mean the absence of pain. Pain will diminish or disappear if and when it's no longer needed. Healing from a spiritual perspective may include accepting pain as part of the perfect process. If you say you want perfection, you will get nothing new, because you're already perfect. Spiritual perfection is made up of many things that seem imperfect. Poor health is one. In actuality, it may be just a part of the perfect process of the Universe.

If you have a physical illness and want to know which scenario dictates your condition, do what you can to heal your physical or emotional self and become more aware of your Spiritual Self. Then thank God and accept the result. When you are living your purpose, you will not change. If your purpose is to be an inspirational figure experiencing illness for the benefit of the whole, then your condition is appropriate. Adopt a passive and more accepting attitude, instead of one full of frustration and anger because of physical discomfort. Accepting does not mean submitting. Never give up. If you do you won't know when the purpose for your condition is served.

Pain is of the body, suffering is of the mind, and neither is of the spirit. The great yogi Ramana Maharishi remarked to his followers during his excruciatingly painful battle with cancer, "Yes, there is pain, but there is no suffering." Highly spiritual people do get sick. This proves God doesn't pick and choose who gets ill and further proves that illness is part of the perfect process. This allows us to experience peace in comparison. When you have pain but don't feel as victimized as previously, you'll have reached a new level of consciousness. You are now realizing your power and transcending at least part of the physical illusion.

Application: Weathering the storm

If you're in pain, it may help to think of it as the surface of the ocean during a storm. If you try to maneuver a boat during this storm, you'll have great difficulty. Your entire being will be involved in fighting the violent waves. An awakened spiritual being understands that the surface of the ocean is but a small part of her. She can remain safely in the calm under the surface, aware of what's above, but not dwelling or fighting in it. An awakened spiritual being does not need to dwell in pain. She knows it would be unwise to weather the storm from the surface.

Material pain

Sometimes holding on to pain is the same as holding on to material possessions. Pain can help us feel alive and connected to the physical world we are so afraid of losing. People who hold onto pain in this manner distract themselves from facing their fear of losing their identity. Some people may unconsciously feel that if they lose their pain, they lose their life as well. I call this "material pain." I've seen people who are actually afraid, usually unconsciously, of losing their conditions. They hold on to it as if it is a personal possession. They talk about it as "my bad back," or "my ulcer." By not understanding their powerful creative abilities, they unconsciously program to keep these possessions. In such cases, finding out who they really are by understanding their eternal nature is usually all they need do to remove their fear and alleviate their condition.

A final comment on healing. There is nothing wrong with going to the doctor. Traditional medicine mostly treats symptoms and deals with crisis. Alternative health systems usually help prevent illness and restore the body's natural ability to heal. Both have their purpose, and everything you can do to help yourself should be considered. A medical health professional might assist you by alleviating your physical or emotional symptoms, so you can focus on internal healing.

> *"I will heal them and reveal to them abundance of prosperity and security."*
> *Jeremiah 33:6*

Application: Creating health

When attempting to heal a physical condition, envision the end result you desire. Consider, for example, someone with a broken leg. Using the Theatre Technique, imagine watching whom you desire to help heal enter the stage from the left. Now imagine the ball of white light, full of energy, spinning slowly and powerfully. Watch the light flatten out and begin to move downward until it reaches the person's leg. After the light passes this part of the body, imagine that the leg is now completely healed. See it that way. Accept it as fact. Imagine the person dancing, laughing, and thanking you. Get up from your seat, go to the right of the stage, and move toward this person, greeting and embracing each other in the center.[8] This is the new blueprint you've created that will be quickly manifested if it is best for everyone involved.

---

[8] These *two* people can be the "new" and "old" you.

Abundant Wisdom

Wisdom is the opposite of judgment. It is the understanding that you and God are one. It is the realization that the illusions of the world are what they are, and what you thought you *knew* is also part of that illusion. It is knowing who you really are, and that you need nothing.

Wisdom is the understanding that you have the ability to create your world with the power of the Universe within you. Wisdom is also recognizing that all the positive and negative life experiences we create are part of a natural duality inherent in the perfect process. Wisdom is recognizing that you are a perfect creation participating in this incredible process of re-discovery. Consciously serving the Universe by sharing Love is the result of wisdom.

The credo of Bukkyo Dendo Kyokai (The Society for the Promotion of Buddhism, Japan) states, "Though he should live a hundred years, not seeing the truth Sublime; yet better, indeed, is the single day's life of one who sees the truth Sublime." You need only accept the possibility you don't know everything. After that, true wisdom is realizing and accepting that you don't have to.

Become connected to the Universe, and your wisdom will become Divine wisdom.

Abundant Wealth

If you were given riches and material goods from birth, you wouldn't appreciate them as much as if you acquired them later in life. Many people born rich fear losing what they have. They were taught that material goods are the best measure of self-worth. They may dwell in an obscure rationalization by believing, "If I lost what I have, it would hurt me more than it would someone who never had it, because they wouldn't know what they were missing."

If you're in this situation and feel this way, realize *you* may be the one who "doesn't know what you are missing." Not having hit yourself with the hammer, you may not fully appreciate how it feels to stop. There is no reason not to enjoy your illusory wealth now, since we all experience everything eventually. Just keep it in perspective.

Myth: "Money is the root of evil."

This is not a truth in the spiritual reality. Some of us have made it a reality in the physical world, because we believe not everyone can have a lot of money. We simply assume there's not enough to go around. Whatever God has made available to one, God has made available to all. No one is more deserving than another, and if it is money you want to experience, then you can have it.

Remember two things if you desire more money: (1), Don't ask for it; create a picture of yourself already having it; and (2), create a picture that includes what you really want the money for. Don't picture yourself sitting on a pile of money. Picture yourself behind the wheel of that sports car you've always wanted.

Money is part of the physical world and therefore not a spiritual reality. Since we currently dwell in the physical world, we can't ignore money because it's difficult to do without. However, it's not difficult to keep it in proper perspective. You can have what you desire. If it's money, nothing by God will prevent you from having and enjoying its benefits. Problems arise when people become too caught up in finances, allowing it to be all-consuming. Money is only a part of the physical experience, and "you can't take it with you." Once you can enjoy it or leave it without feeling loss, you've realized its reason for being. Money may mean many things to many different people, but it is not evil.

Doing business with the Universe

Myth: "In business, someone wins and someone loses."

Spiritual abundance is most important when you think of business. If you believe someone else must lose so you may gain, you're not alone. But you're not spiritually correct.

Many business people will tell you, "It is a dog-eat-dog world out there, and you have to fight to survive." This is their reality. If they are good enough salespeople, their experiences and apparent successes will confirm their belief that they must "eat or be eaten." This attitude leads to unhappiness, because it prevents a sense of oneness with all. Doing business as a spiritually awakened being means working in a way that everyone wins. If everyone wins, each person satisfies their financial needs and spiritual desires, creating real happiness. Wealth gained by helping others is true gain.

Love what you are doing, and do what you do with Love. One of the best ways to show people you are a loving person is to smile, and do it sincerely. See God in each person you do business with. Besides being good business, it allows you to share your true self with the people you work with. Most, if not all, of my business success can be attributed to my "customers" liking and trusting me. I always had the best of intentions and they felt this. I wanted to help them as well as myself.

It's good business to feel a sense of unity with whomever you do business. If you operate in a manner that disconnects you from employees, customers, or co-workers, you'll remain disconnected from your true self. I would rather feel Love through helping others than guilt from taking advantage of their trust. Corporations would be wise to embrace this ethic. It's in their best interests. They should realize that bringing peace and happiness to their customers and employees brings happiness and prosperity to management and the bottom line.

Giving people what they want has always been good business. But are you giving them what *they* want or what *you* want them to have? If you don't treat them fairly in business, you slow your own spiritual development. You both are the same person, in a spiritual sense. If you adopt an attitude to provide people with products and services as if you were selling them to God, you might do things a little differently. You might realize you are not being fair and feel guilty about it. In this case, you are wise to listen to your guilt. It is dissonance created from being "off center."

Your true nature is Love. When the missing feeling of Love is replaced by a feeling of guilt, it says you are not doing the spiritually correct thing for all involved. None of this means you can't make a lot of money. It means you should help people get what they want. When you do, you reap the benefit of getting what you want. Everyone wins.

Application: Affirmations for business

Center yourself and repeat the following:

"I can and will help others. I have a talent and an ability that can serve my true purpose and all of humanity."

"I am serving others as if I am serving God."

"When I do business with Love, I am rewarded by the Universe."

Working with Love

If you understand your spiritual purpose in relation to the work-place, you can find a job you love, or love the job you have. Working with a feeling of purpose brings all the financial rewards desired and a greater sense of personal satisfaction and spiritual growth. Do you feel you're in a business that provides a comfortable living but takes advantage of others? If so, either find a more loving way to do your work or find a new job that lets you be the real you.

If you work for someone, you may feel you don't have to care or try as hard as if the business was yours. If so, you're missing out on a more fulfilling physical experience. You may eventually feel you are wasting your life until you find a business of your own. You may believe that the owners are winning, and you are losing, because you are "doing their work."

Don't be fooled by the capitalistic nature of society into believing that you should eventually work for yourself. When you work as a spiritually conscious being, you are always doing something for yourself and for everyone you touch. We are a system of spiritual beings, working together to re-discover ourselves as One. Your job is only a *part* of who you are. Don't take anything in the illusory world too seriously because it may dominate your life. Just do the best you can each and every moment. Your job is how you make your living, not how you make your entire life.

Martin Luther King Jr. said, "If a man is called to be a street sweeper, he should sweep streets even as Michelangelo painted, or Beethoven composed music, or Shakespeare wrote poetry."[9] Imagine a world where all people were happy with what they did and respected every other individual's contribution in making the world a more loving place. Imagine no one needing feel that his or her job was better or worse, or more or less important, than another's, knowing there was a spiritual purpose for everyone's existence and job with enough resources for everyone to prosper.

Application: Affirmations for your job

Repeat the following in a centered state:

---

[9] Martin Luther King also said, "there are no undignified jobs, just indignity in the way certain jobs are regarded."

"There is no job more important than mine; we are all One."

"I am doing my job with Love."

Intuition in business

Myth: "Successful people are lucky."

Using your intuition is another important factor in doing what you do better in business. Some of the most successful and brightest stars in the business world use their intuition to help make good business decisions. Conrad Hilton used his intuition to decide where to build his first hotel. John Paul Getty used his intuition to decide where to dig for oil. There is no mistake; developing your connection to your Higher Self can and will help you in every aspect of your life. Work hard to develop this connection and remember the old business maxim: "The harder I work, the luckier I get."

Why use only the five physical senses to get information and answers to your questions, when you can also use your additional five "psychic" senses.[10] Using all ten gives you twice as much chance to make the best possible decisions. When you practice centering yourself, you will not only develop your relationship with God but your inherent creative abilities. You realize more of what you naturally are, an intuitive Genius!

Affirmations

Center yourself and repeat the following affirmations:

"All the world's beautiful gifts are for me to have, enjoy, and share with humanity."

"When I make love to someone, I am connecting with, and making love, to God, and it is beautiful."

"I accept everything the Universe has to offer."

"Whatever I truly desire, believe, and accept as already existing, I can own and enjoy."

"I am happy, healthy, wise, and wealthy, and this is so."

---

[10] Your five physical senses have corresponding "natural" psychic senses.

Lesson VI summary:

It may be more desirable to be broke and happy than rich and miserable. It might be even more fun being rich and happy. You can have everything when you accept that whatever you really want has already occurred and is within you to realize. You can lay out new blueprints for your body and the Universe for whatever you desire to build. If you are centered, and what you desire is purely for the best intention of your soul and all of humanity, it will be manifested for you. Whether you desire happiness, health, wisdom, or wealth, you can have it all.

The Universe gave us everything. Since giving and receiving are the same act, by giving to others we are giving to ourselves and creating abundance in everyone's lives.

Create abundance, create Love.

Technique #10

The Chakra Balancing Technique

Purpose:

To awaken, energize, balance, and refresh the seven major energy centers (the chakras) in the human body in order to re-vitalize the body by increasing its energy flow.

Application:

Make sure you've practiced the previous techniques before doing this one, so the energy you feel will be familiar. Do this technique once every month or whenever you want to feel more balanced and alive.

Procedure:

There are seven major chakras in the body (see the diagram below): the root chakra, located at the base of the spine; the spleen chakra, located between the root chakra and the navel; the solar plexus chakra, located just above the navel; the heart chakra, located behind the heart; the throat chakra, located in the throat area at the base of your skull; the brow chakra, located between your eyebrows; and the crown chakra, located on top (and inside) your head.

In a sitting position, center yourself and take a deep diaphragmatic breath in through your nose. Imagine breathing in a beautiful white light, directly into your root chakra to a count of seven. Hold the breath for a count of three, feeling a swirling energy building within your root chakra. Then exhale to a count of seven through your nose, allowing the image of the swirling energy to remain in your root chakra. Keep breathing into this chakra, imagining that every time you do, the energy grows in size and becomes more powerful. When you imagine the energy emanating from within and now surrounding your outer body in this area, repeat the procedure for the spleen chakra while remembering to keep the picture of the swirling energy in your root chakra alive.

Now connect the two energies and allow them to swirl around in a synchronized manner. Repeat this process with the rest of the chakras. As a final image, feel all the energy centers balanced and alive. Now sit quietly, imagining these energy centers glowing with power, connected and spinning slowly together in unity.

Now imagine that with every inhalation you receive powerful energy from the Universe through your crown chakra. This energy enters from the top of your head and moves down through the chakras to the root, and then slowly up and out the crown chakra on your exhale. Imagine building energy within your system with every breath. While continuing this process, silently add the affirmation, "I am receiving all the energy I can handle and use." When you are finished, close this technique with an affirmation of thanks before counting out from one to five.

How it works:

Sometimes there is a blockage of energy within one or more of the body's energy centers. Energizing and uniting the chakras can restore the flow of healthy, healing energy. White light is a symbol of energy (and enlightenment). By concentrating on and filling each chakra with this power, you create a balanced flow of energy in your body, allowing yourself to feel more alive. The finishing affirmation of thanks helps close the crown chakra and contain the energy when the technique is completed.

Additional comments:

Don't use this technique at night before going to bed; it's intended to wake you up and energize you. Make sure you imagine all the centers spinning slowly with energy in the same direction, as one unit, and all connected to each other. This is also a good technique to relax and energize yourself before participating in a sporting event. If you decide to do this, try to complete it no less than an hour before the event.

You're likely to feel completely passive and relaxed just after you complete this exercise, but should begin to gain energy with an hour.

Relax, You're Already Perfect

Technique #11

The Channeling Technique

Purpose:

To learn and develop energy transferring ability, for both hands-on healing (for self and others) and distance-healing.

Application:

Use as needed to heal yourself or others near you (hands-on) or away from you (distance-healing).

Procedure:

After doing the Chakra Balancing Technique, imagine energy is pouring in from your crown chakra and out through your brow chakra in the form of a powerful white light, tinged with a little blue. Now imagine this healing light going into your hands. Feel the energy in your hands, which may be a tingling sensation or warmth. Imagine your hands beginning to glow, radiating with energy coming in from your crown chakra. Once you feel this energy in your hands, place your hands on your subject to allow this energy to flow through you. It's not necessary to put your hands where there is pain or where healing is needed; the energy will know where to go.

Once you can do this, all you need do from now on is desire to heal in this manner, center yourself, and imagine energy coming in from your crown chakra into your hands. You may then apply your hands to yourself or to someone who desires your help, allowing the flow of energy to enter the body. If the person you want to help is not with you,

you can use the Theatre Technique and imagine him or her in the center of the stage with you next to them. Imagine energy coming in from your crown chakra, going to your hands, and being directed into the person. After you do this for ten to fifteen minutes, envision the final image of the person totally healed. See him or her happy and thankful.

How it works:

Energy is received through the crown chakra, which has been called the "gateway to heaven." Once you have your chakra open, you can transfer energy to anyone anywhere on the planet. Physical laws are no limit. Once the energy is channeled, it will be received by its recipients when and if they want it, and if it is in their best interests. They do not need to be aware you are helping them.

Additional comments:

You do not create this energy and should not be drained by doing this technique. You act only as a channel and allow it to flow through you. If you do this correctly, both you and the person you help will be energized. If you feel drained afterwards, you are trying to make it happen, instead of allowing it to happen.

Lesson VII

We Are Eternal Beings

*"Immortality is the one concept you can bet your life on,
whether you believe in it or not!"*
From the 'Directing the Universe' seminar

There is no real death, only an end of the purpose for our physical bodies. When you understand it's only your body that dies, and that you are an eternal being, you'll have no need to fear physical death, or anything, for that matter. Since there is no real "end," there is nothing real to fear. This should allow you to relax. Energy spent on unnecessary worrying can now be spent on discovering more about yourself and your true nature and purpose — discovering how to live!

If you choose to believe in a limited existence, you'll most likely see the world and your purpose in it as meaningless. As a result of living with feelings of fear and isolation, you may experience anxiety, depression, despair, self-pity, and loneliness. Even worse, you may feel nothing at all.

Again remember that God is both perfect and eternal, so everything created by the Universe must be, as well. Anything we see that appears limited in duration is not created by the Universal Mind. It's an illusion created by the individual mind. All illusions are created for experiential purposes and are part of the physical world — death is no exception.

Myth: "After it's over, it's over."

There are two philosophies regarding existence. The first says we are just bodies: physical beings that are born, live for a while, and die. The second says we are eternal, that our essence lives on. Only our physical body dies. Which thought gives you the most comfort? Which is peaceful and associated with Love, and which perpetuates fear? Most people who embrace the first philosophy (consciously or unconsciously) fear death. Some may even welcome it if they hate or fear life. Until you awaken, it is understandable to fear death; fear and death coexist as illusions.

Plato said a philosopher prepares for death by considering the possibility of eternity, which frees the soul to contemplate upon it. If you decide to accept a belief in your eternal nature, you can free your mind to create more happiness for yourself through a more pleasurable life experience. If you choose to not believe in immortality, you'll at least benefit from the perfect process of the Universe through the experience of physical death (everything has a purpose). Physical death itself allows us to experience our fears at the end and, immediately after we pass, the jubilation of knowing we are eternal. It may appear the caterpillar is dying until it awakens in a different form to a new beginning. You, too, will eventually realize your physical death is only a transition.

As physical manifestations of the Universal Energy, we have the powerful ability to create any reality we choose right now. Because we have the power of the Universe within us, the illusions we create seem real, and all too often consume us. They seem so believable, as real as a dream seems until we awaken. And so it is that until we awaken spiritually, we must remind ourselves of the illusion of mortality.

The thought of death seems both real and painful. Relax, my brothers and sisters and accept the perfect process as it is. It will one day result in your knowing. The question is, when will you know? Through free will, your mind can decide you are ready to remember your true nature as an eternal, spiritual being. This will be a blessing after living so long with the fears of life and death. To create the most happiness in your life now, I suggest you believe in life after death, and "cross that bridge" when it comes.

Death is a conception of the individual mind. When we accept ourselves as the everlasting beings we truly are, we lift the burden of a death sentence. God does not work in mysterious ways: it all makes sense when you look at it through perfect eyes.

> "... and deliver them who, through fear of death, were all their lifetime subject to bondage."
>
> Hebrews 2:14, 15

Truth: The spirit knows

When we awaken to our true nature, we become more consciously aware of our Spiritual Self and free ourselves from the limiting beliefs that are part of the physical world. While you are spiritually sleeping, the illusion of mortality is the warden in your imaginary prison. The One Spirit knows it is eternal and indestructible, and it is therefore completely fearless. When you are connected to your Spiritual Self you, too, will become fearless, as you will be able to feel the wisdom and peace of the truth.

What would be the purpose of our lives if we were not eternal beings? We would just go through the motions day by day, unmotivated except to consume as much of the material world as we could. We would do this in an attempt to fill the void that results when we don't remember our true nature. It shouldn't be too surprising that people who don't see the big picture are abusing the world's resources. If they knew the truth, they would hold the environment sacred, and not feel the need to consume and control everything to distract from the fear of losing their physical self.

There may come a time when the Universe has no use for this physical world. If we destroy the planet before we are ready, the entire process of evolution will have to be repeated. No thanks.

Life is not short, it is forever. Eternity is our true nature. If you have trouble feeling this, try the following exercise.

Application: Loving eternity

Center yourself and think about the two choices of belief: mortality and immortality. Which gives you the feeling of Love in a centered state? Since fear is not pure Love, and Love is our true reality, anything that creates fear in us is not real. When the feeling of blissful Love is associated with the idea of immortality (or any other idea you desire to clarify), you can allow this feeling to tell you the truth.

That frees you to share peace and Love with all those you touch.

If you don't yet feel the truth of Love, you are not centered. Continue to practice the Basic Centering Technique, and all the other techniques in the book. Practicing centering techniques is necessary to enhance your connection to the Divine, so you can experience this powerful feeling of spiritual Love on command.

Were we here before?

Myth: "There's no such thing as reincarnation."

It isn't important to believe in the idea that you have had many lives. I don't believe in reincarnation. But then, I didn't believe in it in my last life either. (Sorry, I couldn't resist.) Reincarnation is a confusing concept. If we are eternal beings, we never really die. So how can we be reincarnated?

Only the physical form perishes. Our souls persist. Once we have no need for our present bodies, our souls move to a different dimension (not a different *location*), one beyond the comprehension of our physical mind.[1]

What would be the purpose of the need to come back to this dimension? Why not just get it right the first time? Having to "keep coming back" may not seem like perfection, but there is no time or space in the spiritual world. It's as if time, as we understand it, freezes, though we are still able to move around and do what we normally do. A lifetime is but a flash of your permanent existence. Actually, without time to measure, there are no "lifetimes," since everything happens simultaneously. The past, present, and future all exist *now* in the spiritual world.

All existences in the physical dimension are available to fulfill specific purposes your Higher Intelligence has for you. When you "get it right" or "experience it all," your soul moves on to another dimension, if it chooses. Or, it can return to help others. There is no rush, however. Your soul has all the time in eternity.

The movie *Groundhog Day* illustrates the purpose of returning to get it right. If you saw the movie, you may enjoy this interpretation. If you haven't seen it, do so, as it is both enlightening and funny.

Actor Bill Murray plays a self-centered, grouchy "Scrooge"- type TV

---

[1] But this otherwise elusive concept is accessible to your individual mind when it links with the Universal Mind as a result of your mastering your centering abilities.

weatherman.[2] The character becomes caught in a time trap that causes him to relive the same day again and again. At first, he's scared and confused, and doesn't know what to make of it. Once he's sure it's an ever-repeating existence, and that he'll never die or suffer any repercussions from anything, he decides to take advantage of his predicament and experiment with many of life's available experiences. He experiences fear, anger, greed, lust, gluttony, sex, crime, pain, and even death. He believes his goal is to "land" his pretty TV producer, so he makes every effort to trick her into bed.

After a while, he realizes he's not going to win over the producer. When he encounters an old man who dies, his new goal becomes to do everything he can to prevent the man's death. To try something different each time the same day recurs. Ultimately, he accepts it's not within his ability (or his purpose) to save the man. The next day, which begins as a repeat of the previous day, the character is happier, more relaxed and poised. He begins with a speech that inspires and motivates his fellow beings. Instead of gloating about the speech, he immediately leaves to begin a series of "errands," which range from helping people through small deeds to preventing a boy's serious injury and saving a man from choking. He does these things without thinking about them, as if he were simply *acting naturally* and doing the best he can for himself and the people around him. He appears to enjoy helping others.

We can assume he didn't feel this enjoyment before. He was ornery and miserable. Finally, without effort and after humbly accepting thanks from the people he touched, he wins the heart of the producer. The day after this "perfect" day, he wakes up with her next to him, which is not a repeat of all previous days. He finally wins her heart without trying to be anything but his true self. He has ended the seemingly endless series of days lived over.

This story illustrates what our many existences in this dimension are all about. We continue to re-discover ourselves, through life's many experiences, until we realize that we can just be the loving people we really are. Instead of living many lifetimes to realize this, the movie character lived it in one day. From a spiritual perspective, there is no difference between one day and one full life (or many lives).

---

[2] Mr. Murray also played Scrooge in an updated version of A *Christmas Carol.* I wonder if his mind keeps choosing this theme for him to experience for some purpose.

The character always had the power and ability to live that perfect day. He needed only to find out, by trial and error, what *his* perfect day was. He did this by comparison, learning what it was like to live and experience many pleasurable and painful situations to know and express his true self as a loving, caring being. Every time he found something right for him, he kept that piece of the puzzle by repeating the behavior, letting go of the rest until all pieces fit perfectly.

We each experience this process and are in a time warp, of sorts, to find our true selves. We each have a purpose — a different perfect day (and life). When we live ours, we help others to the best of our ability, consciously serving ourselves, God, and all other souls in the incredible journey of re-discovery. Eventually, we each will live in the eternal bliss of Love. To move your soul in that direction, find and live your perfect day, today.

One more interesting note about the movie *Groundhog Day*. At one time I'd have been unable to see it from this perspective, and would have enjoyed the film for entertainment purposes alone. When you begin to remember your spiritual nature, your viewpoint of the world around you changes. *When the student is ready, the teacher appears.* The teacher can be in many different forms: a person, place, a book, even a movie.

Application: The perfect day

Using the Theatre Technique from Lesson V, imagine and create your perfect day. First consider how you would create this day knowing that you are an eternal, indestructible, and invulnerable being. Believe you are without worries and fears. Imagine knowing you are powerful and completely happy. Don't concern yourself with what you would be doing, or who you would be with, only how you would be doing it. Before creating your day, think about the things that are part of your life now. Keep what you believe describes your most loving qualities. Imagine changing anything you would like to change.

When you're ready, imagine watching the "new you" enter the stage from the left,[3] completely loving, caring, and happy. Imagine how other people greet you, showing only Love. Watch as you share Love and create happiness with them. When you are ready, let the

---

[3] Remember that whether you are using the Theatre Technique to bring in an "old" you, or a "new" you already changed, always have the figure enter from the left of the stage, which represents the future.

old you get up from your seat in the theatre and enter the scene from the right of the stage. Move to the middle of the stage and merge with the "new you." Try to experience all the wonderful emotions and feelings that go along with this day. Change the scene to wherever you desire and mentally go through a complete perfect day minute by minute. Be creative; there's no limit to what you can do or be on this day.

Once you have an idea of what it feels like to experience your perfect day, try to re-create this in your actual life. When you see people, let them see you as a loving, caring being, and allow yourself to motivate, inspire, and touch their lives through your energy and Divine presence.

Your beliefs about reincarnation should be determined by the level of comfort you feel with the idea. Believe whatever you wish as long as you feel relaxed and happy. If you choose to look further into the phenomenon of reincarnation, read some of Ian Stevenson's work where he describes, from a scientific perspective, what appears to indicate actual evidence for it's existence. This may help you increase your belief system, so you may more easily accept immortality as a reality.

Even though I read and truly enjoyed Dr. Stevenson's work, I remind you that you need only center yourself to understand most of life's mysteries. Only minds that lack confidence in their own abilities need to hear "evidence" from experts and science to tell them what to believe. You are the expert! Open your mind and heart, and feel the truth.

If you believe in past lives, and have some problems in this lifetime, you may want to consider receiving past-life therapy counseling from a professional. It's possible your problems in this life originated elsewhere. Through this type of therapy, you may find a certain painful pattern repeating itself. By simply recognizing it, you may become enlightened enough to break the pattern forever. Dr. Brian Weiss's books offer some experiences of people who have benefited from past-life therapy.

Who chose whom?

Myth: "I didn't choose to be born."

The client who accepted this myth as his reality believed that because his parents "willed" his creation, he was just a product of their desire to have a child. He felt less worthy than they, and lived in their shadow. He also felt his only purpose in life was to be their son. This belief manifested itself in depression we eventually linked to feelings of insecurity, which resulted from his not remembering who he really was and why he was here.

Our spirit is eternal, which suggests a state of existence "between" physical lives. If you did "come back" to this dimension, it would be because you (your soul) did so to fulfill the intended purpose for the life just past, or, if it was fulfilled, for another purpose. If in this between-lives state we are ready to return to the physical world, we must decide two things: our purpose for the upcoming incarnation and the best form to pursue that purpose, including who our parents or early family will be.

The idea is how best to move toward Love. Our birth choice is not only to best help us accomplish our purpose, but to assist our parents in their self-discovery as well.

If you have children, you may have heard one of them arrogantly say to you during an argument, "Hey, I didn't choose to be born!" Now you can tell them, "Oh yes you did!"

I've worked with clients who believed their parents were physically and/or emotionally abusive to them as children. It's most important for people who experienced this type of childhood trauma to understand how they, better than anyone, have the capacity to feel Love when their pain stops. Their souls might even have chosen this childhood experience for that purpose. Whatever happened to us, we have the power and ability to transcend the past and the physical illusion. We can awaken to live in the now as spiritually enlightened beings, never feeling like a victim again.

Hell, and the devil

"The only devils in the world are those running around in our own hearts. That is where the battle should be fought."
Mahatma Gandhi

Myth: "I'm afraid I am going to hell."

Could there be a "bad" place we might "go" when our physical self ends? Many people believe if they sin they'll go to hell when they die. They are partly correct. Hell exists, but it's not a place you go when you die. It's not punishment for your sins; as there are no sins in God's eyes.

Hell exists in this dimension. Hell is the life you can choose that includes unnecessary suffering as a result of a disconnected body, mind, and spirit. Throughout this book, I have attributed many qualities to the group known as the Sleepers. In a sense, they are in hell. They are unconscious of their real essence. If you think of hell as the opposite of heaven, then realize our personal hells occur when we're not in touch with the heaven within us.

Living in hell is living within the illusions of the physical senses, instead of the reality of Love. What are the penalties and pains of being in hell? The only punishment of a hellish life is unfulfilled happiness.

Don't be afraid, nothing bad happens to you in your personal hell. It can simply be considered an experience before awakening. It's still part of the perfect process, and when you realize you are no longer in hell, you *know* you are in heaven, and know it by comparison. It's impossible to describe the freedom of peace after liberation from hell. You can only know it by experiencing it for yourself. Anyone who knows this feeling will probably tell you that, after realizing hell was an illusion, they never felt happier, more secure, or whole. If you never taste true Love, you can never know how much you'll like it.

The devil resides in hell, but it is not a person or entity. The devil is fear. "He" is part of people's illusory, limiting belief systems. By "listening" to the devil, one is actually living (following and reacting) out of fear. In *Bible Mystery and Bible Meaning,* author Thomas Troward relates it was Jesus who preached in the synagogue of Nazareth that "everything which keeps us from enjoying our life to the full is [what the Bible calls] the Devil." Until we awaken, the devil resides within us all, restricting our potential to enjoy life.

Belief in the reality of the "negative" experiences confronted in the physical world is temporarily necessary (Lesson II). But it's we, through our own power, who can free ourselves from the bondage of these illusions. It is our free will that allows us to create our devil, and keep us in a living hell. The same free will gives us the power to walk through the imaginary bars that imprison us. As Karl Marx said (in another context), "You have nothing to lose but your chains."

Addictions

There are many distractions that alleviate the pain of not being connected as body, mind, and spirit. One way we distract ourselves is to attach ourselves to what the physical world has to offer and become overly reliant on that to satisfy our desires. This is called an addiction. Addictions are illusory distractions of the physical world that temporarily mimic the satisfying feelings we can achieve without them.

When you're attached to something, it's hard to give it up if you believe you give up the relief that goes with it. Until you realize this relief is temporary, and that you already have something within you more real, powerful, and satisfying, you'll be controlled by your addiction.

The process of creation does not stop after this life. If we are addicted to something in the physical world, it's possible we may not realize we've passed from this dimension to another, and continue to create and maintain an addiction. Addiction to anything but Love is complete absorption in the physical world. It can temporarily fix our mind in the physical illusion, even when our bodies no longer live. This absorption can be like a false god that keeps the mind in darkness as the soul waits. In this case, those addicted to something from the physical world may remain spiritually asleep even after they pass from this dimension. They may even repeatedly reenact (in their minds) an addiction they had in the physical world until they are helped "into the light" by the Universal Mind. Or until they awaken by remembering who they are.[4]

Addictions in this life or beyond can be very painful experiences. But they are not permanent and nothing to worry about, as all minds eventually awaken. Even addiction has a purpose — to help the addicted person realize the illusion and know the reality of true freedom when the addiction is overcome. If you have any addictions, you can help yourself by understanding and living the lessons in this book.

You may also consider therapy. Address this problem now because addictions take you further away from true Love and happiness. Although you'll eventually remember the truth (as unknowing leads to knowing in the perfect process), why not enjoy it in this lifetime? If you

---

[4] This idea is somewhat similar to the traditional concept of hell, but it is no different than the hell we create for ourselves on earth.

drop out of the school of consciousness, you'll want to go back until you graduate. Why wait?

Soul mates

Myth: "We each have one soul mate."

A common belief is that as eternal beings, we have a soul mate who we need to find life after life. This belief has caused many marriages to fail, because people constantly questioned whether they had found the one "right" person for them. This belief is also responsible for perpetuating a fear that we will lose our only true loved ones.

The idea of a single "right" person for each of us is unjustified. It limits our ability to realize that we are all connected to one another. In truth, each and every person is a loved and "right" one. Given our present very limited (albeit purposeful) physical abilities, it may be difficult to understand what it is like to be all loving to every soul. You'll eventually begin to recognize and remember this feeling. It will be a familiar feeling since you've experienced it many times before, possibly in other dimensions. You can experience at least parts of it again by developing your new skills, which will benefit you for the rest of your life.

Our souls recognize souls from a different dimension who can help us remember ourselves. We have many soul mates, not just one or two. Some people believe we are reincarnated again and again into the same group of souls. When we move on, we re-unite with this group. This is partially true. We experience these same souls until our purpose to re-discover ourselves is realized. We then re-unite with God and *all* souls, for they are all part of ourselves.

For the time being, we find comfort in the souls we know. They are familiar to us and help us pick up where we left off in another lifetime. We remember and recognize them easily, so we don't have to live each life without help. They help us remember things we've already experienced (and do not desire to repeat) and allow us to share Love more easily.

Our soul mates might even be something other than human beings. They might be a career, an area to live in, a vacation place, and so on. Anything that helps us remember who we are can be considered a soul mate. In this respect, it's understandable why some of us have strong desires to do certain things, visit foreign places, or seek out specific areas to live that seem comfortable to us.

Affirmations

Enter a centered state and repeat the following affirmations:

"I exist now, always have existed, and always will exist— for all eternity."

"As Love is eternal, I am becoming more loving every day, because that is my true nature and will bring me the most happiness."

"I shall never be afraid again. I am light. I am Love. I am forever."

Lesson VII summary:

The only thing that ends when we die is our doubt about our eternal nature. God could not create something that doesn't last, so the true nature of ourselves is everlasting, indestructible, and immortal. Belief in your eternal nature helps you remove fear, remember Love, and enjoy peace and happiness. Not believing produces fear and prevents a truly enjoyable life. Anything you see or feel that is not Love is an illusion.

You are life and you are Love — forever!

Technique #12

The Passive Centering Technique

Purpose:

A partial list of benefits for passive centering includes: healing of the body, mind, and spirit, increased concentration, improved memory, improved creativity, a heightened sense of awareness, lengthening of life, and connection to the Spiritual Energy.

Application:

Do this fifteen to twenty minutes, once a day, for about a month. Use it in addition to the Deep Relax Technique, if you have the time. Otherwise, practice the Deep Relax Technique for a month and then begin the Passive Centering Technique for an additional month. After your initial training, use the Passive Centering Technique as often as you desire.

Procedure:

Sit in a comfortable position, with your legs crossed to create a bio-energy connection. Center yourself and still your mind. Repeat the sound "OM" with each exhalation and whenever you have a distracting thought. Hum "OM" out loud for an entire session. In another session say "OM" silently. Choose the method that most relaxes you.

How it works:

"OM" is a "mantra" used to stop distracting thoughts. It's also a trigger, or reminder, to relax. The sound is associated with the crown chakra and suggests liberation to spirituality (the purpose for opening the crown chakra). This peaceful and passive session will help calm your mind and create a healthful state of being. Just being connected to the Spiritual Energy helps you heal your body, mind, and spirit without conscious effort.

Additional comments:

Distracting thoughts are natural and nothing to be concerned with. They decrease with practice. Although some of its effects may be apparent right away, the benefits of this technique will increase over time as you practice. Many people do all their praying and programming in this relaxed state and see great results. If you are a passive, or introverted individual, you may find this technique appealing and effective. More extroverted and aggressive types may benefit more from methods such as the Theatre Technique, designed for people who prefer to "get more involved." Keep the piece of the puzzle that fits, and let go of the rest.

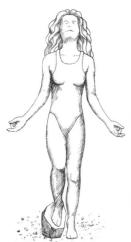

Lesson VIII

Love Yourself

"I myself am the enemy who must be loved."

C.G. Jung

How can you expect anyone to love the real you if you don't love yourself? If you don't love who you are today, do you really want to be with someone who loves you that way? Rediscovering Love is our purpose. This includes the Love within our self. If you don't allow the Love within to reveal and express itself, you won't be able to share it and truly enjoy life.

Some people are alone. I don't mean by themselves. They are alone in the sense of not having their best friend with them all the time — their own self.

Be your own best friend

Wouldn't it be nice to have a friend who never lets you down? One you can trust? You can be your own best friend, and once you realize this friendship, you can enjoy all your "other" friends as you would yourself. When you love and befriend yourself, you are not as demanding of others, and you will not feel disappointed by them. You will know you have everything you ever need within you. All your other relationships will thrive and prosper, because you put no pressure on others to give you Love.

By finding your positive attributes and getting to know and appreciate yourself, you'll learn to love yourself and become your own best friend. To help you find a friend in yourself, try this exercise.

Application: Becoming your own best friend

Set aside a time to be alone every day. Have fun by enjoying a hobby you like or simply taking a walk. Don't get too caught up in the activity. Just try to consciously enjoy spending time with yourself.

Use the Personal Paradise Technique from page 85 and be alone in this wonderful place. Feel yourself as one with nature. Run, jump, sing, dance, and have a great time by yourself. Spending time this way helps you look forward to being with your "new" friend, and enhances your connection to the Universe.

Myth: "I need someone to love me."

"Seek not abroad, turn back into thyself for in the inner man dwells the truth."

Saint Augustine

If you don't love and enjoy yourself, you rely on others to bring you love and enjoyment. This is not fair to them or to you. Getting too hung up on what someone else can do for you cheats both you and the other person out of the sharing experience. If you want to experience others, it should be to see what they have created and how they live. Share their experiences (as God does) with them.

In this way, you are better able to remember more about yourself through them. By communicating with others, you vicariously experience more of the physical situations the world can offer. Without others to assist you, you would have to live all those experiences by yourself. There are too many experiences for you to re-discover who you really are without help. This is why the Almighty created more than one of us.

The truth is we already have within us all the Love in the Universe.

Distraction by attachment

Love by attachment to another is not true Love. It is infatuation with one of the physical world's illusions. If you are constantly "looking for love" outside yourself, then, as the song goes, you are looking for it in "all the wrong places." A love for a person or object outside oneself lasts only as long as the person or object. Anything that does not last eternally is not real. When you turn within and realize your true essence, you will remember that you lack nothing in your personal greatness. You'll then know you are worthy of giving and receiving true Love to and from the people around you. When this happens you no longer *need* Love from others, but *desire* to experience more Love by sharing it with them.

Before we awaken, many of us are under a fear-created delusion that we need someone else to love us or we will not feel Love. Although we all experience some type of love from others in our lives, if this is our only measure of love, it will inevitably lead to loneliness or emptiness when it's gone. Clients who have experienced this have told me they were suffering from a "broken heart."[1] Love from within can't be broken. It is indestructible and permanent.

If you don't love who you are, you might, even unconsciously, wonder why the one you are with would love *you*, an "unlovable" person. You would then begin to question their motives. I've seen many people undermine their relationships (and the possibility of a good relationship) out of self-doubt and insecurity. This sabotage may come in the form of jealousy, which can be devastating to a relationship. You are more likely to be jealous if you have low self-worth, thinking that the person you are with would certainly be interested in finding someone better than you.

Sharing true Love from within uplifts you and helps others to experience and remember Love as well. They see it and feel it from you. The Love you give (and receive) will be pure from the One Spirit. It is easy to share Love when you are a centered individual. You express it effortlessly, energizing yourself and the people you touch, as this energy is the one true essence and life force. By expressing and sharing Love, you become more Godlike.

Application: Expressing Love

Some expressions of self-love include: healing yourself and help-

---

[1] When one of an elderly couple dies after a long marriage, chances are great that the surviving spouse will die within one year. They feel as if a part of them has died and will never be complete again, losing the will to live. In essence, they are creating their own death.

ing others to heal themselves, reconciling with those you feel the need to; and performing acts of kindness, such as giving of oneself in the form of assistance, a gift, or affection. Take time to express yourself in at least one of these ways every day. You'll help yourself and the people around you realize a wonderful, more satisfying life.

Another way to practice the art of expressing Love is to let someone help you with something. This gives them the experience of knowing Love by making another's life a little better. It assists them in effecting their purpose by helping another through effort and contribution. You'll be doing them a great favor. It feels good to give. Allow people to give to you, and accept those gifts lovingly, just as you would desire them to accept yours.

Myth: "Putting yourself first is selfish."

Selfishness suggests receiving without giving and hoarding for one's own self. Sharing Love with others is the most unselfish thing you can do. Do it sincerely from the heart and you will be rewarded many times over. *There is no other way to start experiencing the sharing of true Love with others than to begin with self-love.*

Application: I love you

Do the Basic Centering Technique and tell yourself, "I love you," again and again. This not only reinforces your belief, but helps your entire body system get a moral boost and encouragement to fight for itself. You'll be telling your system that you believe you're worth fighting for.

Delusions of grandeur

Self-loving people feel total confidence within. They have no need to receive approval from others. Self-love is not to be confused with vanity or grandiosity, which are qualities of the ego. People who have to "show and tell" how great they are usually feel they need recognition and reassurance from others.

Loving who you are has little to do with what you have or the way you look. These should not be determining factors that measure your self-worth or your conditions for self-love.

Truth: You can't hide from yourself

I know someone I'll call "Andy," who has a lot of money. Andy constantly tells others how rich he is. When some of his employees commented on how nice his sweater was, he replied he had enough sweaters to wear a different one each day. When you first meet Andy, you might think he's the most delightful and happy person you have ever seen.

When you get to know him, however, it becomes apparent that Andy's presentation is only a facade. He doesn't have many friends. And though he is close to his family, he's a very lonely person. To compensate for his lack of self-love and self-worth, he projects an image he believes will get him respect and love. Andy has many positive attributes and a special gift to offer others, which has not yet been realized (Lesson V). These attributes are hidden by his outward appeals for attention, which come from his lack of self-love and self-acceptance.

The universal purpose is to re-discover and share Love. If you do not have a true feeling of self-love, it will be more difficult for you to consciously pursue your purpose in this life. It has been said that you can't do the proper job without the proper tools. To serve your purpose, Love is the only tool you need.

Self-love as a guide

Once we are able to feel Love inside, we know what will feel right to others. True Love is a universal feeling and a spiritual truth for all. If you are a centered spiritual individual, you can use self-love as a guide for how to treat other people just by listening to your own feelings.

Truth: Love heals

When we are totally loving of ourselves, something wonderful happens to and around us. Our auras begin to radiate with joy. People who are either naturally able to see auras or trained to see them[2] could tell you a lot about a person's present condition just by observing the energy field around her.

When you are ill, your energy field appears dull. When you are happy

---

[2] You can train yourself to see auras by staring at an object or person. Using your peripheral vision, observe the colorful field around what is in front of you. If you are interested in pursuing this further, read a book on aura reading.

and full of Love, your energy level increases and becomes brighter. When this happens, people and animals will want to be near you; this energy is attractive and makes them feel good. By becoming more loving of yourself, you are allowing others to feel more Love, in the form of energy, which they then radiate back to you.

You can use the energy in your own field and the energy of the Universe to heal yourself and others. There is an unlimited supply of energy just as there is an unlimited supply of Love. And so, when you love yourself, you are more consciously doing God's work because you are assisting others to live, enjoy, and re-discover Love. This is a very important role in the human drama; one you can easily play without much rehearsal.

Practice this exercise to develop your natural abilities to energize and heal. This may give you an idea of just how powerful and loving you can be.

Application: Grow Love

Using the Channeling Technique described in Lesson VI, take a plant and hold either the plant or its pot between your hands. Now imagine a blue-white light pouring in from your crown chakra (atop your head), going into your hands and radiating through the plant from your right hand to your left hand, in that direction. Allow this energizing and loving process to continue for approximately fifteen minutes. While you are healing the plant, envision an image of a healthy plant. Do this once a day for a few days and you'll begin to see a healthier, livelier plant! If you're interested in seeing how well this works, put two plants next to each other and energize only one. You can perform this same exercise with fruit (which will last longer and be healthier), water for drinking or cooking, animals, and, of course, people.

Be self-reconciling

One of the reasons we may not love ourselves is that we may not see ourselves as being "lovable" or worthy of Love from others. Maybe we feel we have not been as "good" as we could have been in our lives. Maybe we believe we have hurt people and feel guilty. We may even believe we have hurt ourselves. These are limiting beliefs. What you've done in the past is what allows you to find the person you want to be today.

In Lesson III we discussed how we do not need to "forgive" anyone, as everyone's spiritual nature is perfect. Instead, we should come to an understanding of others using the process of reconciliation. We also need to reconcile with ourselves. If you feel that you have hurt yourself or someone else, reconcile this by understanding you did the best you could under the circumstances.

After this, do your best, on the physical level, to reconcile with anyone you feel you hurt if you believe it necessary and beneficial to everyone involved to do this. Spiritually, you cannot hurt yourself or anyone else. But in the physical world, *you* may suffer from guilt in certain situations because you don't understand the perfect process. This unnecessary suffering blocks your energy and prevents your happiness.

Application: Making amends spiritually

It is important, while you are in this dimension, to reconcile any past pain with yourself and others.

For resolving guilt:

Practice centering yourself and then use the Theatre Technique from page 127. Create a new image of yourself, one that you can be proud of. Bring the "new" you and the "old" you together in the middle of the stage. Have the new you tell the old you that everything is perfect and understood. Now combine into the new "absolved" you, feeling and accepting that this is the truth.

For reconciling with others you feel you have wronged:

If you can't reconcile on a physical level, enter a centered state using the Basic Centering Technique and imagine him standing in front of you. You can imagine any setting you like, or use the Theatre Technique as above. Tell him you love him, and ask that he understand you. Make sure you imagine seeing and hearing him smile and telling you he understands everything and accepts and loves you as you are.

This is more than just an exercise. If you are centered, you will actually communicate with each other at the spiritual level. Your thoughts are sent to the Universe as energy, and when the other person is ready, he or she will receive your message. Now understand, accept, and love yourself because you have done what you needed to do. Have faith.

Use this exercise if you feel someone has hurt you, and you would like to reconcile with them. Just center yourself and use the same process. See them explaining themselves to you, and see yourself understanding, accepting, and loving them. It is not necessary to tell them why you felt hurt (although you can if you like), as you are the cause of your feelings, and that is something you need to remedy by understanding from within.

Be self-accepting

*"Being loved by God, manifesting itself as love for God,
can only be experienced on the basis of self-acceptance."*
Otto Rank

Self-*acceptance* is understanding the physical limits of our present state of being, as opposed to self-*realization*, which tells us how wonderful we are in our true spiritual sense. Self-acceptance is the recognition we are limited by both human nature and the level of understanding obtainable with our human minds. This does not make us less than perfect, because we need to temporarily experience these limitations in order to remember who we are. This we discovered in Lesson II.

By becoming self-accepting, you allow yourself to relax and be the best you can be at that moment. This removes any pressure you may feel because of unreasonable images or expectations you've placed on yourself. Self-acceptance is knowing you are who you are, and that you are perfect just that way.

Accept who and where you are *today*. This includes your present beliefs, abilities, and level of spiritual development. If you desired to move a mountain with only the power of your mind, truly believed that you could do so, and accepted that the mountain was already moved as a result, it would be moved!

However, if you believe that maybe *one day* you will be able to accomplish this feat, then maybe *one day* you will, though probably not today. To take a practical example: Suppose you know of someone who has healed herself from an undesirable condition similar to yours, using only the power of prayer. You decide to do the same thing and ignore the advice of a medical doctor. This decision may reflect a non-acceptance of who and where you are today. The person who healed herself may have been more spiritually conscious than you at this moment and more skillful in utilizing certain self-healing techniques.

Self-acceptance is self-monitoring. This means living and accepting each moment in your life as best you can given where you are. It is living and loving your life with the understanding that every moment in it is purposeful. You do not have to be anything besides who you are now. Love yourself today.

Lesson VI told us that part of wisdom is accepting you don't have to know everything. This is self-acceptance as well. Accepting what you don't know will lead you to knowing. By opening yourself to mystery, you'll make yourself available to surprising possibilities otherwise invisible to you.

One way to effectuate the process of self-acceptance is to appreciate the physical body's physical limitations for what they are — purposeful illusions. These illusions, once recognized, will free you from limiting ideas of who you really are. Thus, if you believe you are God in this form, would you believe yourself to be imperfect? Or would you know that what you see is a charade, a purposeful project, or "projection." What you are seeing is a temporary human form, designed to help you re-discover your true self. Believing is seeing: *believe* that you are accepting of who you are, with all the apparent physical limitations necessary for the process of re-discovery, and *see* yourself as the perfect creation!

Application: The acceptance letter

Sometimes we express ourselves much more effectively in letters than in speech. Center yourself and use one of the passive forms of meditation, such as the Nasal Deepening Technique described at the end of this lesson. Remain in this state for fifteen or twenty minutes. Immediately after you finish, write a letter to yourself. Write how you are now ready to accept your physical limitations as part of the whole of perfection. Write that you accept everything about yourself that seems imperfect, and that you love the fact that you now realize the power and ability to understand this. Accept all you have done or think you should have done in the past. Tell yourself that you will never question or doubt yourself again. Add a comment or two about how much you would like to make a commitment to love yourself unconditionally from now on. Add anything else you would like to say.

This interesting exercise may be emotional for you as well. Notice all feelings you experience during this process. Allow yourself to feel any pain and pleasure, to clear a path for a new beginning.

If you like this exercise, continue it by answering the letter. Read it as if it had been mailed to you, and then answer it with thanks, saying anything you want to say back to yourself. If you do this well, there will be an actual communication taking place between your physical self and your Higher Self.

Myth: "People can hurt your feelings."

Emotions other than Love can make us feel vulnerable and insecure. It's these illusions that allow us to feel hurt through the actions of others. It is not possible for a person who has nothing but Love inside to be emotionally hurt by another. Part of self-acceptance is understanding your unpleasant emotions for what they are — comparisons so you can know Love. Be self-accepting: accept your insecurities and vulnerabilities as purposeful illusions. You create your emotions. They belong to you, and no one else. Only you can choose to let others hurt your feelings. Choose to *not* let it happen.

There is also the possibility you may feel "hurt" by others when they don't act the way *you* want them to act. They may not be doing anything to you, but your perception makes you to feel "let down." If this is the case, look deeply (while in a centered state) at your expectations of the other person. See if you believe the way you would like them to act is truly best for you and best for them. Many times, you'll find that your desire for them to be a certain way comes from your lack of self-love. The truth is always within, so feel it and be free.

Myth: "If she really loved me, she wouldn't have hurt me."

"We must learn to penetrate things and find God there."
Meister Eckhart

It's hard for some people to comprehend why one who loves them would hurt them. People seem to hurt others either because they are spiritually conscious beings who feel that what they are saying or doing is the loving thing,[3] or because they express the hurt they themselves feel in the only way they know it. Either way, understanding is part of accepting the way things are. Understanding helps you control your reactions and your life. And understanding is the key to moving past the hurt. Know there is always a purpose for whatever happens, and that everything leads to Love.

People who are not spiritually centered sometimes abuse others to deal with their own pain. They usually do this unintentionally or unconsciously. They are ignorant; not stupid. They don't know why they do the things they do or how to stop. Once again, the fault lies in their belief system. They may be lonely, not realizing that they have Love within them, and strike out from frustration.

They believe they can't control themselves. Or they may feel their actions are natural, stemming from family experiences.[4] Not knowing any other way, and maybe even believing what they are expressing is love, they express their pain onto the people around them. There is nothing sadder, as all involved suffer needlessly. Remaining unhappy prolongs their suffering in the physical world.

Even the incredibly painful experience of abuse, be it childhood, marital, or even self-inflicted, is still part of the perfect process. As difficult to see as this may be, such abuse will lead those involved to a better understanding and appreciation of what peace and Love are by comparison.[5] It is in just these types of difficult situations that we must penetrate things to find God's perfect process at work. If not, it will be all too easy to lose faith, get caught up in the illusion, and remain unhappy. Remember, God would never let God's perfect creations suffer; there is no suffering in the spiritual reality.

Self-love and self-acceptance are the first steps in removing the pain and loneliness left by the actions of others. If you or anyone you know is abusive to another, help them understand and encourage them to get help, so they too can enjoy their life more.

---

[3] Awakened centered people know that spiritually, they can never hurt another.

[4] This is commonly the case in child or spousal abuse, as the abuser was often abused as a child.

[5] This is not to suggest accepting being victimized. Self-love also includes self-protection.

Truth: We are never alone

Sometimes people do not remember that they can turn within to God and realize they are full of Love and connected to the "spiritual family." Loneliness to them feels like the only reality. It is a feeling so powerful that some people will do almost anything to alleviate the devastating pain that goes along with it.

A centered individual doesn't feel lonely. Being centered and connected in body, mind, and spirit creates a loving feeling. You know that you are secure and safe. This is very important because once you attain this level of Love, you will have attained real Love. You will know you can feel it whenever you desire, and never be lonely again.

In counseling, I've met many drug and alcohol abusers who reported loneliness as one of the key "triggers" to their addictions. To deal with the disconnectedness they feel to themselves and others, some people turn to drugs. Others do the unthinkable, as the following story reveals.

Several years ago while vacationing with my first wife,[6] I received a phone call that her brother had killed himself. We were devastated, to say the least. It was the most painful experience of our lives.

My brother-in-law's girlfriend had just broken up with him, so he put a shotgun to his head and ended his pain. He left a note saying he couldn't stand the thought of being lonely any more. At the age of thirty, it was his first serious relationship. When it ended, he must have feared the loneliness he had known before and didn't want to face again.

There was a time in my life after this happened that I believed I felt as lonely as he had. I understood why he hadn't wanted to live. The difference between us was that I knew that I would recover. He didn't. Although this thought didn't ease my pain, I knew the pain wasn't going to last. I knew it was not real in a spiritual sense. I felt that I still loved myself, and that no one could ever take that from me. Through my brother-in-law, I vicariously experienced what it would be like to not love the person I was. It was the most painful thought I ever had.

Through tough times we need to see the light or we may lose faith. I included this story only so others can benefit from his "sacrifice." A

---

[6] The stress of this event led to the termination of our marriage. We are both happier now: the perfect process once again demonstrated through a divorce that was very painful at the time.

purpose can always be found in even life's most painful events.

Your spirit guide

For those of you who feel alone, there's someone that you should meet. It's not a person (at least not in the sense of our physical form), but another energy force that's always with you — your spirit guide. Some refer to their spirit guide as a "guardian angel." Some consider this entity another dimension of themselves, and they are correct, as we are all of the same spirit. But this is a real entity, and a valuable and loving friend for life and beyond. It doesn't matter what you call this presence, if you realize it's available to help and guide you for as long as you dwell in this dimension.

There are many gifts from your spirit guide. Your guide sends valuable information through your intuition. If you're awakened, you'll be more receptive to this information. You can turn to your spirit guide in times of trouble for energy and comfort. Discover a friend for life. Meet a powerful energy force by employing the Spirit Guide Realization Technique at the end of this lesson.

All conflict is self-conflict

Myth: "Conflict is unavoidable."

I've heard this myth a couple of times as a rationalization for what is happening in these clients lives. They are victims who refuse to accept that they create their reality, and that conflict does not have to be part of it. Loving yourself creates a harmony of body, mind, and spirit within. When harmony exists, there is no room for discordance, or conflict. Conflict can exist only with doubt. Universal Love is without any doubts.

When you're self-loving and accepting of the principles in this book you will become totally secure and feel no need to argue your beliefs with anyone. Anything you hear that is not Love will not affect you. You will be centered in Love only, and nothing will be able to pull you out to create dissonance.

A centered individual can't feel conflict with another. Only the challenger has conflict, or there would be no challenge. Conflict between individuals occurs only when two people oppose each other. Like Love, the centered being opposes no one.

Love yourself — love the world

Are you ready to experience a world where we all love ourselves? It would be a more spiritually fulfilling and happier world. The next lesson will help each of us create such a world.

Affirmations

Center yourself and repeat the following silently:

"I am discovering what it is like to be my own best friend."

"When I love myself, I have more Love to give to others, and this makes the world a happier place."

"As I gain Love in myself, I lose fear and loneliness forever."

"I cannot feel Love and dissonance at the same time. I choose to feel Love."

Lesson VIII summary:

The only way to consciously re-discover true Love is to love yourself. You will *desire* but not *need* anyone else's love, which allows you to realize the gift that others have to offer — shared Love. By loving yourself and knowing that Love is your true nature and that of the Universe, you'll get closer to remembering that you, everyone around you, and God are all the same.

Don't be afraid to love yourself. It is not your true character to be a victim of humility. Once you accept the realization of who you really are and why you are here, you will be more awakened to the powerful loving co-creator you truly are.

The most incredible joy available is to share the Love you have inside. To become a spiritually awakened being on earth is to adopt, as your purpose, re-discovering and sharing your Love to help yourself and others experience God.

As we love ourselves, we love God.

Technique #13

The Nasal Deepening Technique

Purpose:

To reach a deep level of centeredness for healing while developing concentration ability. The Nasal Deepening Technique also helps balance your left and right brain activity.

Application:

Do this technique as needed to help you improve concentration, creativity, and the ability to remain aware of what you are doing in this state of mind. It's also a good passive technique for healing physically, emotionally, or spiritually. Use the Nasal Deepening Technique when things seem too chaotic, to gain a sense of balance.

Procedure:

For improved concentration, awareness, and healing:

Imagine breathing slowly (to an estimated count of seven) in one of your nostrils and out the other. Then breathe in the second nostril and back out the first. Continue for approximately fifteen to twenty minutes. If you forget what you are doing or get distracted, bring yourself back to the exercise and continue. The more you improve at this, the greater will be your ability to concentrate and relax.

For improved creativity and balance:

With your eyes closed, actually hold each of your nostrils closed one at a time for a full breath. Breathe as deeply and slowly as you can.

How it works:

This is a modified yoga technique. By concentrating on your breaths, you will be using breathing as a type of "mantra" to train your mind to be more focused and centered. When you hold a nostril closed, you make sure you're breathing through only one at a time. This is done to access each side of your brain, to develop a greater sense of balance, and to relax after too much left-brain activity.

Additional comments:

Imagining breathing through one nostril at a time is a passive, but challenging technique to sustain for fifteen to twenty minutes. If you want to see how well you're doing, try counting the breaths. On the first slow inhalation, count one. On the exhalation, count two. When you reach ten, count backwards toward one. If you get lost, begin again at one. When you are able to count from one to ten, and from ten to one three times straight without losing count, you've gained great control with this exercise. Don't get frustrated if you can do only a few breaths before losing your place. Just keep practicing.

Technique #14

The Spirit Guide Realization Technique

Purpose:

To realize you are not alone but with someone who can advise, support, and help you any way you want, whenever you wish.

Application:

Use in conjunction with the Theatre Technique when you're healing yourself and/or others. Imagine your guide aiding the process and sending energy to any new image you have created. While in the theatre, your guide can also assist you in some very creative ways, such as offering questions for you to ask the person you are attempting to heal or have already healed.

Use your guide any way you desire, especially when you need answers to questions. In a centered state, ask him or her something and wait for the answer. An answer may "pop" into your mind and will be the most beneficial one if it is associated with Love. Also, you can meet your guide in your dreams, using the Lucid Dreaming Technique, and ask questions or share experiences in that type of conscious dream.

Procedure:

Begin with the Basic Centering Technique, and then the Theatre Technique. Tell yourself that at the count of five your spirit guide will walk onto the stage. Count slowly, and at the count of five imagine your spirit guide walking out from the left wing (from your perspective) onto the stage and standing on the upper left part of the stage. If you have difficulty imagining a person, simply imagine an energy force in the shape of a body. If you cannot see a person or energy force, try to sense it through feeling. Once you begin to sense this presence, try to add a face, whatever face comes to mind. Once this "person" is there, go to the right part of the stage and begin to move toward each other to a slow count of five. Greet and embrace this entity in the center of the stage at the count of five. Ask him or her any question you desire and listen for the answer. Then ask your guide to sit behind or next to you from now on whenever you enter the theatre, and to be available any time you desire. Tell whoever it is that you will call on him or her from time to time when you need help. Imagine your guide saying, "My pleasure, happy to be here!"

How it works:

Your spirit guide is a very real energy force who's here to guide you in your journey of re-discovery. She talks to you whether you realize it or not, through dreams, feelings (intuition), and during your centering exercises. By placing a face to this energy, you may realize a better connection to her, and gain more awareness that this force is always with you. As you allow yourself to be more aware of, and be in conscious contact with, your guide, you are more able to take advantage of the many gifts this "being" has for you. Always ask this entity for advice, as your spirit guide is a connection to and part of your Higher Self.

Additional comments:

Before doing the technique for the first time, think about who you would like your guide to be, and see if the same person shows up. Either way, if you are centered, whoever shows up is right for you. If you are uncomfortable with your guide, repeat the exercise and choose someone else. Once you get results with your guide, don't try to change him or her.

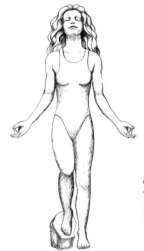

Lesson IX

Surround Yourself With Love

"Oh, what a world that would be!"

Barney the dinosaur

All the lessons up to this point have told us we are the powerful creators of a world of our own conception. Why not create a new world today, just the way you want it to be? Fill it with the kind of people you want to be with; a world full of Love, emanating from you and touching everything and everyone you meet. You *can* create this world today and let all of humanity benefit from your creation.

Everything we are is based on relationships. Relationships between ourselves and loved ones, our environment, our work, and God. Relationships even include those between us and our own emotions, thoughts, and belief systems. We create these relationships. If we don't like one we're in, we can recreate it. This includes our job, our home, our religious affiliation, our friends, and even our family. Ultimately, there is no reason why we can't be surrounded with Love.

How do you relate?

We discussed the relationship between you and God in Lessons I and II and between you and Love in Lesson III. How you relate to your belief system was covered in Lesson IV; and recognizing your purpose in Lesson V. Lesson VI discusses your relationship to work, play, and health. In Lesson VII we remember our relationship to eternal essence. And in Lesson VIII, the relationship between you and your inner self is discussed. All relationships affect your life in different ways. In this lesson, we'll assess an important one: the relationship between you and your environment. This includes the people in your life and the physical world.

People relationships

The people you associate with are a reflection of who you are. If you don't like who you see in the mirror, you may indeed have to change who you are. But you may also want to change who you are *with*, or how you are with them. They are in your mirror, as well.

Close friendships

Relationships with other people allow you to share experiences and perspectives, so that all can remember who they are. Mutually beneficial relationships serve the process of re-discovery and they serve Love. In a more loving world all people remember who they are, and why they are here.

Once you are wholly conscious of your Spiritual Self, it will not matter who you're with; there will be no one who can bring conflict in your life. You'll enjoy everyone for what they can offer. During your spiritual journey, however, it is not wise to surround yourself with those who slow your progress and divert you. If the people you call your close friends bring you "down," consider ending those relationships. Instead, be around people with whom you can share positive energy, Love, and respect.

For each person in your life, ask yourself, "How do I feel when I am around him or her? Am I happy, energized, secure, and loving toward them, or do I feel belittled, angry, frustrated, and drained?" If you find some are in the second group, one of you must change if you want to be happier. Or something should. You may bring them down with your own negativity, which they reflect back. Or they may really be a problem for you. For a guideline to help you decide if you should end a relationship, try this exercise:

Application: Love them or leave them

There are two ways to deal with a problem close to us. Either change your relationship, or avoid the person. Changing a poor relationship is better than avoiding it since we can always remember more about ourselves when we're with others. Here are a couple of suggestions to help you do this.

First, try the "reconciliation" exercise described in Lesson III. If you're having difficulty in an important relationship, lovingly tell the other how you feel, and why you want to feel differently about your relationship. Let him know you don't blame him for your feelings. Tell him how much he means to you, and how much you would like to improve the relationship because of your good feelings for him. You'll be amazed how some loving honesty can transform the relationship immediately.

When telling others how you feel, avoid the, "you make me feel..." trap. Let them understand you want to feel different and that you believe they can help you with this. After the discussion, the relationship may improve simply by your coming to an understanding as to why they act the way they do. This can happen if you listen with your heart, not your head. You may find one of you took things personally with no basis for doing so.

If you don't want to do the above exercise face to face, or would like to add to it's effectiveness, try communicating with the other person at the spiritual level using the "Making amends spiritually" exercise (Lesson VIII). See the other person as God. Imagine him or her explaining things from Love's perspective. If you're centered and truly ready to hear them, the messages received will be from the Universal Intelligence.

Once you've completed the process of reconciliation in this manner, you'll have planted the seed in the physical world. If you believe in what you've done, it will grow exactly in the way you imagined if it's in the best interests of all involved. Trust the power of the Universal Energy to move it in the most beneficial direction. You'll have done your part by removing any physical blocks.

If you find that you can't change a relationship, then avoid it or leave it. You don't do yourself or another much good if you are not helping each other at this time. "Love it or leave it."

Relationships with emotional partners

Myth: "It's never as good as in the beginning."

You may be attracted to someone when you first meet but it may be on a physical level mostly. When the excitement of that original feeling fades, you may feel something is wrong with the relationship. In actuality, you only misunderstood the meaning of relationships.

As in all types of relationships, the purpose of romantic relationships is *to learn who you are in relation to the person you're with.* Our potential for knowing ourselves is hidden, awaiting discovery.

Your emotional relationships are part of the perfect process. They're no different from experiencing peace in relation to stress, satiation to hunger, and so on. Romantic relationships offer opportunities to re-discover and share Love by experiencing compassion, kindness, unity, and acceptance, as opposed to the negative feelings and situations that you've had before or after. All experiences help you define and re-dis-cover who you are.

Romantic relationships also help us remember self-security. As physical beings, we often feel vulnerable when these relationships begin. We may feel exposed, because we don't want to lose our new "partner." But our Spiritual Self is invulnerable, and we may learn how invulnerability feels compared to the illusion of insecurity.

By understanding the purpose for romantic relationships and accepting the pain along with the pleasure, you stop placing demands on, and judging, your partner. This allows you to enjoy each moment of a relationship for what it brings. And, being nonjudgmental is more God-like.

Myth: "My partner completes me."

God didn't need to create more than one human being to experience the physical form. That would have been enough if it were the only purpose for our creation. The true purpose is to find out who we are. Our true nature is Love, which must be *expressed* to enjoy, we need others to do this. Our "partners" help us share Love, which lets us experience what that feels like.

As valuable as others are for our re-discovery, they don't "complete" us. We don't need Love from another if we have Love within and for ourselves. The Love we share with others helps us know what Love is by experiencing and letting others experience it as well.

I've heard many happy couples say, "I found the person who completed me." I've also counseled individuals who once believed this, and now feel "incomplete" because of a break-up. They placed the burden of becoming whole on another rather than themselves, and felt the pain in doing so. We are not incomplete in any way. When we look at another as someone we need to complete us, we assume a position of inferiority. As such, we don't acknowledge that the Almighty already gave us everything. Feeling incomplete limits our ability to realize true happiness.

Lesson VI reminds us that you'll look forever if you look for true happiness outside yourself. The happiness you think a companion brings you is no different than any other illusion. True happiness, just like true Love, is attained only from within. When you place demands on others to make you happy or complete, you ask the impossible. Once you're loving and happy with yourself, you allow others to see and share the real you, the *whole* you: body, mind, and spirit.

When you remember you're whole as a spiritual being, you are secure in every relationship. You benefit from what others bring you, but never feel you'd "lose" something if things went wrong.

Truth: You can never lose Love

There's a way to know if you are a completely awakened spiritual being. This is a challenging concept that must be read with a very open mind. Otherwise, you'll miss the message because of fear.

You'll completely realize yourself as a spiritual being on earth if you stop worrying about losing anything. This includes your money, job, home, and even your family. If you understand the true purpose for relationships, you realize they only add to your life; they can't take anything away from it, because you're already whole. They *can* allow you to more fully experience Love, of course. But the pain felt by their loss is part of the illusion so we may know True Love. Once we know spiritual Love, the illusion, along with the pain, vanishes.

In a story from the Bible, God asks Abraham to sacrifice his son to prove his faith. This story illustrates the lesson for Abraham to understand that he lost nothing real by his sacrifice. There's no feeling of sacrifice in a whole spiritual being. Once he acknowledged his Spiritual Self was the only true reality, he could offer his son[1] and move past material possessiveness as an illusion of the physical world.

While I understand this truth from the Universal Spirit, I would never want to lose my loved ones. This book is part of my journey, as well as yours. I realize and accept my physical limitations, and understand they are part of the perfect process. I accept that whatever I experience at any moment is purposeful. Thy will is being done.

Argue with love

Myth: "People don't argue in a good relationship."

Many client couples I see feel there must be something wrong with their relationship because they argue.[2] They believe they shouldn't quarrel with their mates. When they do, acceptance of this myth often causes things to be blown out of proportion. Arguing isn't necessarily the problem. But the purpose for the argument may be.

When you argue to win, you are certain to lose. It doesn't matter if you "won," because you leave the other person with less energy and self-worth. This is poison to a relationship. It doesn't matter if the argument is between you and your spouse, you and your boss (or employee), or you and a stranger. The point of disagreement is resolution, not winning.

During your spiritual development, realize there's nothing harmful about arguing and challenging, *if* it is done with Love and respect. A healthier way to argue, one that will help you move in a more spiritual direction, is to show Love by communicating properly during a disagreement. Really *listen* to what is being said.

One of the most common complaints I hear is that a couple's relationship lacks communication. The best advice I can offer here is that *each person should listen to one another as if they were listening to God.* Doing so promotes real listening and respect.

---

[1] As the story goes, once he realized this, the sacrifice of his son was not necessary, and he was spared.

[2] I find it amazing that many couples come to therapy with the expectation that the counselor is responsible for saving the relationship. They say, "We'll give him a try, and if it doesn't work, we'll end the relationship."

Application: Communicating with Love

A simple and therapeutic exercise that shows Love and respect is to listen without judgment.

Practice mutual listening. Do not interrupt, think about what you're going to say next, or decide whether or not you agree with what they're saying. Simply listen with the idea you want only to understand their message. After they've spoken say, "Let me see if I understand..." and repeat in your own words what you think they felt or meant. This exercise helps you learn how to *feel* what the other person is saying, using your emotional ability instead of thinking and arguing with your head.

You may not understand or agree with what the person is trying to say, and that's perfectly OK. You don't always need to. It's the interest and care that's most important. The need to know and agree with everything is part of the ego and the physical illusion. Everyone is different. Accept those differences. If you find yourself getting angry, it may help to say, "I love this person as I love God. She and God are one."

If you don't know or agree with what the other person says, it could be because of insecurity stemming from your not knowing who you really are or what you believe. If so, relax and find the real you.

When you remember you're are a spiritual being in a physical form, you'll no longer need to argue. There'll be no reason, because there'll be no conflict. When you remember you are only Love, you no longer feel a need to defend your beliefs. Love is universal and needs no defense. *There cannot be an argument with only one person involved.*

A final thought about romantic relationships. Never try to make the other person who *you* want them to be. A spiritual being accepts others for who and where they are in their spiritual development. He or she realizes that they, too, are a perfect creation, working through and helping the perfect process.

Relationships with children

"You may become a Shakespeare, a Michaelangelo, a Beethoven. Yes, you are a marvel."

Pablo Casals

If you've had the incredible experience of watching the birth of your child, you've at least glimpsed at unconditional Love. You adored this little person with all your heart and put no demands on him or her. You expected nothing from the infant and just enjoyed how he or she made you feel. This never has to change! Somewhere, sometime, someone gave you the message that you *must* do this or that with your children and they must, in turn, act a certain way or they're not "normal."[3] From that point, you probably judged and compared everything they did to others, forgetting the purpose of their creation was to re-discover yourself in relation to them.

If you rely on your children to make you happy or fulfill your unrealized dreams, you place an unfair burden on them. It's only when you realize this that you can share a peaceful and loving relationship with them.

Your belief system was heavily influenced by your parents when you were young. Your parents (or caretakers) were God to you, just as you are God to your children. They want to trust, listen to, and respect you. The images you help create allow them to develop their own belief systems. Are you acting like the Higher Intelligence would, with unconditional Love and understanding? Are you empowering your children, or are you trying to control them?

The ideas you give your children are what they'll believe, at least until they can think for themselves. If you've done your job with Love, you can feel secure they'll have an easier time remembering and following their purpose in life, without having to first create healthier belief systems.

How would you want a stranger to treat your children? Should you treat them differently? Some people think they have the right to treat their children differently than they'd want others to, because these are "their" children. You don't own your children. They are souls, just as you, who belong to the Universal Energy. When you treat them as personal possessions, you show them disrespect, which helps create a perception that they are neither equal to nor as important as you.

That's not to say your children shouldn't respect you. This is desirable for both parties. It means you should help them create a sense of

---

[3] When new parents bring their children for checkups, they are told how their children "compare" to others and what is "normal."

individuality, self-esteem, and sense of security. Most important, help them experience unconditional Love.

Respect from your children is not automatic. It is subjective and decided by their impressions. You earn their respect by letting them see and sense you as a kind, loving, respecting, and secure person. They'll more easily develop the same qualities. Don't try to *appear* perfect. You *are* perfect in your natural state; you needn't try to be anything.

Many people raise their children like they were raised. The problem with this is that we, as one evolutionary unit, are growing and re-discovering who we are every day. If we live in the past, we stunt our growth and that of the rest of humanity. Your parents did the best they could given their strengths, weaknesses, spiritual development, and belief systems. Accept what they did as part of the perfect process in your life, whatever happened. However, you are not your parents. Let your children know who *you* are; you're certainly not the same person you were when raised. Your time has come. You've progressed as part of your experiences. You've developed just from being part of, and connected to, humanity's universal movement toward, and understanding of, spirituality.[4]

Parenting doesn't end when your children are grown. You'll always be the parent and have an affect on your children's lives, even if you no longer have much physical contact. No matter how old you or your children, if there's a message you feel can help, give it. Even if it's simply to say you did the best you could for them at the time. Let them know you loved them when they were young and love them still.

Myth: "Kids are born either good or bad."

Insecure parents afraid to take responsibility for their children's beliefs and development use this rationalization. I've never met anyone who said this who seemed to feel they were doing the best they could. Maybe they were overwhelmed or depressed, and felt they couldn't give their all to their children. If this is your situation, remember you can recreate your life today.

Don't worry about always trying to do the right thing. Forget about

---

[4] The truths I have humbly set down in this book are also part of humanity's spiritual development. Its development and information are part of the heritage and experiences of all past beings.

right and wrong; your ideas may not be in the best interests of your children. Focus instead on expressing yourself in the form of Love and respect. It doesn't take that much effort. It just means accepting yourself and your children as perfect creations, and doing the best you can by listening to your heart as well as your mind.

Myth: "Our children need to know who's in charge."

We confuse the hell *into* our children — literally! Yes, we do need to discipline them, but we need to do it with respect and Love. We needn't allow them to create fear. Often, fear created in children is modeled from the fear and anger of their parents.

If you find yourself getting angry at your children, it could be for several reasons. Perhaps you misunderstood their natural developmental process, or there is too much stress in your life, or are depressed because you're spiritually disconnected. Or maybe you're reliving your unconscious childhood memories through them. Whatever the cause, don't take it out on your children. Over the last few years there's been great debate about what's acceptable discipline and what's considered abuse. God will not decide this for you, because there is no right or wrong in God's eyes. But we were given the tools to decide for ourselves. You "cross the line" if you feel anything but Love while telling your children what they've done wrong or while disciplining them. This is the time to listen to your emotions.

Unconditional Love means loving your children no matter what they do. If you feel any other emotion, such as anger or hatred, you're out of control. If you are out of control at times, get help now before control of your life (and your children) ends up in the hands of others.

When your children are old enough, consider letting them participate in the disciplinary process. Tell them how you believe they should act and why, and ask if they agree. If they don't, weigh the benefits and pitfalls of "bad" behavior until they understand. If you start this process early enough (once they understand what you are saying), it won't be met with much resistance.

Once your children agree on how it's best for them to act, work together to decide proper disciplinary actions if they act differently. Notice I didn't say punishment. A respectful and successful disciplinary action does not have to be a punishment. God doesn't punish; you don't have to either. Remind them that they agreed what would happen if they broke the "rules." Teach them they create, and are in control over, the choices they make. If they choose something not in their best interests, they also choose the possible repercussions. Enforce with Love. I've found this advice to be most helpful to many families I've counseled.

Myth: "We shouldn't fight in front of our kids."

What better way to teach children how to get along with others than to let them see a proper disagreement that uses good communication skills, is respectful and loving, and comes to a mutually happy resolution. You teach by example.

If you can't be civil during an argument, then you should do everything you can to avoid arguing in front of the children. This also means keeping your voices down "in private" when they're within earshot. Agree that if an argument should arise, you'll stop where you are and continue it another time. It's natural to want to resolve things immediately, but that's not necessarily the best for everyone involved.

If you fight constantly, aren't happy, and can't resolve and improve your relationship, you may be interested in the next myth.

Myth: "We should stay together for our children's sake."

People always assume that it's better to remain together unhappy than to have a "broken" home. There are two responses to this. First, from a therapist's point of view, don't be fooled into thinking you can hide your misery from your children. They know, or will know, what's wrong. And you may do them more harm than good by maintaining an unhappy relationship. They shouldn't have to witness unhappiness, because they may believe that's how a relationship is supposed to be. An unhappy relationship is a poor model that they may replicate in the future.

The second response is from a centering session. Each soul is an individual who chose his or her situation before birth. Your children may not want you to stay together and may have chosen to feel the pain of separation. However, since there's no such thing as fate, your free will can create any future. You may be preventing them from accomplishing an experience they chose for this lifetime.

Do whatever you can to be happy in your relationship, so it works out. Realize, however, that it's not in some peoples' best spiritual interests to stay in certain relationships. These relationships will not be saved happily. Don't force yourselves to stay together; you may be helping no one.

Bringing up perfect children

Children are as perfect as you and God. The following additional points will help them (and you) realize this and live a more fulfilling spiritual life.

Provide the information in this book from the time they are born by living it with them. When you think they're old enough, let them read it for themselves. Tell them their purpose is to make the world a more loving place.

Allow your children to believe as they wish. If you want your children to be religious, let them experience your religion and explain the meaning behind the rituals and ceremonies. After you expose them, let them decide if they want to stick with it at that time in their lives. Let them know there's no need for conflict between each person's beliefs, even if they differ. Trust their abilities. It's not necessarily in their best interests to do what you want them to do.

Consider encouraging your children to meditate when they are ready, which should be around four or five years of age. Tell them to sit quietly, close their eyes, and silently repeat a number, word, or saying. Or tell them to simply concentrate on their breathing. You may be surprised how good they are at it. Children are usually more creative and open-minded than adults. They also make better intuitives, because they have not yet been told what's "impossible."

As for education, consider telling your children it doesn't matter to you how they do in school. Advise them to do the best they can for themselves and enjoy their experiences. Let them know they can do anything they want in life, and that you will help and support them in whatever they choose. Assure them you will love them just the same, whether they feel they're successful or not. In your eyes, they will always be successful. By doing this, you show unconditional Love and acceptance. In the process, you experience it yourself. Your children will do what they wish because they want to. Attaining knowledge is stimulating and exciting. They'll choose to learn because it's a natural desire, and they'll do it better with your support, not pressure.

This is not simply a manipulative game of reverse psychology to get them to do better. If you feel it is, read this book again to understand that everything that happens is part of the perfect process. Your children know (or will know) their purpose better than you. There's no reason you can't suggest things to them or encourage what you believe is in their best interests. Just be sure you accept them however they choose to live.

The same process works well for sports and hobbies. It's helpful for children to know the purpose of these activities is for enjoyment and self-improvement. Competition is good, but only as a challenge to themselves, and not for comparison to others. Let them know they can enjoy getting better at what they do. Get the message across that there's no such thing as "failing" or "losing."

Finally, please don't ever tell your children you hate them, or that they're stupid, ugly, too fat or anything else degrading. Destroying their self-esteem will cause much trouble and delay in their emotional and spiritual development.[5]

By adhering to all the principles above, you too will move in the direction of your true Spiritual Self.

Relationships with your estranged family

Myth: "My family comes first."

The client who expressed this myth was trying to make the point she believed in family values. But as we explored that, we found the only thing of value to her was her immediate family. It was then easy to see why she felt her entire world was crumbling when she began to have familial difficulties. It's wonderful to love your immediate family, but believing they're more important than others separates people from one another and from our true nature of unity.

We are *all* family, who appear separate due to our temporary forms and locations. If we remembered this, we would look at and treat each other much differently. We would also take the pressure off our immediate family, by not being so dependent, so we could truly enjoy these relationships for what they offer.

---

[5] The sooner they remember they are spiritual beings, the sooner they will reach true happiness.

I've heard people say, "Other people just don't mean anything to me." Our immediate family is very important; it's the closest to us and allows us so many opportunities for experience. But our immediate family has its worth to us in only one way. Our relationships to "outsiders" operate in other ways. Both kinds benefit us in our journey toward rediscovery.

Myth: "I only need a few good friends."

This declaration was made by a client who seemed to be asking my opinion instead of just making the statement. It was an excuse for not being very sociable. The more souls we enter into relationships with, the more opportunities for spiritual growth. There's no benefit to limiting our friendships. This doesn't suggest that we must love everyone as our own family, but wouldn't it be nice?

Synchronicities

Myth: "You shouldn't care what other people think."

"Coincidences" are creations from our Higher Self to move us toward our spiritual purpose and development. Every person we meet gives us an opportunity to remember who we are, as they've had many experiences we have not. We can remember more about ourselves by becoming their student (and teacher), and by listening and trying to feel what they've been through. This means we can listen and experience vicariously what they experienced in the world and their relation to it. As we do this, we decide if what they experienced was Love. We decide who we are in relation to them.

We can remember something about ourselves from everyone we meet. Many times we come across a particular person or situation that moves us just the way we need to be moved to help ourselves (or the entire world) at that moment. These situations seem like coincidences but are actually purposeful creations or "synchronicities."[6] Our free will decides if we'll take advantage of these "chance" opportunities. The Christopher Reeve example in Lesson I is a particularly enlightening illustration of how this works.

Many synchronicities and signs are available to us. We may get a feeling we should go to a certain place or turn a certain corner, or we

---

[6] This book may seem like such a coincidence to you.

know who's on the other end of the phone before we answer. We meet a stranger who looks familiar, or start a conversation with someone who says something that catches our attention. These situations are created by our intuitive abilities. Synchronicities can be messages from our spirit guide (Lesson VIII) or other sources outside of our conscious aware-ness.[7]

Pay particular attention to these "chance" meetings; they offer great opportunity for spiritual growth at the moment they happen. As you become more aware of your spiritual nature, you'll look for and expect these situations; they'll come to you naturally.

Remember, we are all connected as one Universal Energy. We are all perfect creations.

To better explore yourself in relation to acquaintances and "strang-ers," practice the tips in this exercise:

Application: Bonding with your estranged family

Remember your relationships with acquaintances and strangers offer wonderful opportunities for self-discovery. One beneficial thing to enhance these connections is to give them something of value and ask for nothing in return. It can be in the form of money, per-sonal property, a helping hand, or even just a loving smile. This effort goes a long way and will be remembered by all involved.

Or you can give an "energy handshake." When you shake hands, smile and hold the other persons hand for a few extra seconds to transfer Love from you to them. Imagine Love, in the form of a pink light, emanating from your heart chakra and being received by them through your hand. Look them in the eyes when you do this. It will be as beneficial to you as to them.

The next time you find yourself having "small talk" with some-one you've just met, avoid asking what they do or about their per-sonal possessions. You might judge them by what they have instead of who they are.[8] Try instead, to find out how they feel about their experiences in the world. Try to find the message for you in this "chance" meeting.

---

[7] We may also get valuable information from our dreams. If we learn to remember them and think about their meaning, we benefit from listening to the messages from these "meetings," as well.

[8] In some cultures, asking people what they do when you meet them is considered rude.

Loving difficult people

Myth: "Some people are just bad."

Some believe certain people are "bad seeds" and avoid them. In doing so, they miss valuable information they could otherwise gain from them. There is no spiritual truth to this myth, as bad and good are subjective human qualities. If you perceive someone as bad, you forget the truth about who we all are and what we're doing here.

No one is bad. You can love everyone but don't have to like or spend time with them. Loving is of the spiritual reality (the truth), while *liking* is a judgmental illusion of the physical world. If someone doesn't allow you comfort, you may choose to avoid them. But that doesn't make them bad. Perhaps they're just not right for you at this time. Not liking someone tells you something about who you are or want to be at that moment. It tells you who you are (or want to be) in relation to who they are, or how they are acting. While you are centered, consider why you don't want to be around someone. Then make the best choice you can. You can always change your mind later when you're both in a different and more desirable place.

You can still help by showing Love, knowing they'll move in a more spiritual direction when ready. You also show them the power of Love by letting them see how they can't affect you negatively. Through you, they may remember who they really are and can be.

When completely awakened, you won't "like" or "dislike" anyone. You'll unconditionally love everyone and no longer need to judge them. You'll share and experience Love with them or realize and accept they're in a different place and there's little each can gain from each other at that time.

Your physical surroundings

The relationship between you and your home says something about you. It bespeaks your style and preferences with the choice of possessions you fill it with. If your intuition tells you your home is not most suitable for your soul's purpose (that is, it doesn't describe who you really are), you'll want to move or you'll be unhappy. These are signs from the Universe.

The relationship between you and your material possessions is similar to that between your Spiritual Self and physical self. If you define yourself by what you have and see, then that's all you'll think you are. If you lose what you have, your identity is lost, as well. You live only in the material, physical world. Enjoy the relationships you have with all things in the material world by keeping them in proper perspective. Enjoy your house, car, computer, clothing, and all your other possessions. Just don't let them *possess you*. Realize their purpose is to help you realize who you are in relation to them.

Your relationship with nature

Myth: "Humans are God's most important creation."

Why feel the need to be more important than anything God created? The desire to feel superior is an ego quality that demonstrates lack of understanding of our true nature. Spiritually conscious beings feel no superiority to anything because they realize everything is a part of themselves.

Humans are aware of existence and can experience life in many special ways. This doesn't mean we are more important than an animal or anything else created by the Universe. Other life forms have different purposes. Everything exists because it's perfect that way. We can't survive on this planet without every one of God's other creations. With this in mind, do your best to preserve the world and all its wonderful resources. Just think where human or animal life would be without grass or water.

Lesson IV tells us that our environment is an illusion, so you may feel you don't have to concern yourself with it. This type of thinking is part of your free will but it's not in line with your spiritual energy. If there were no reason for us to be here, we wouldn't be here! When there's no benefit for the physical world, it will naturally cease to exist.

As co-creators with God, we need to do everything possible to maintain this earth, and keep ourselves alive and flourishing. But since we have a free will to create disease, we have this ability to create the destruction of the planet. This wouldn't mean our ultimate destruction since we are indestructible, but it *will* delay our spiritual growth. Why wait?

Affirmations

"I will embrace every person as if I were embracing God."

"I am the creator of my world and am creating Love with all others."

"I am paying close attention to all those I meet, so I can hear their message."

"I love nature and all its inhabitants as I love God."

Lesson IX summary:

Too many relationships are based on what other people or things can do for you. When you understand each relationship allows you the opportunity to realize more about yourself in relation to something or someone else, you begin to realize the true value of every relationship. By appreciating relationships this way, you can more easily sustain and keep them healthy.

In keeping to your spiritual purpose, you have no better choice then to embrace everything God created as you would embrace God. We are in a relationship with everything and everyone on this planet and be-yond. We are all brothers and sisters.

Are you ready to embrace a world with Love?

Technique #15

The Partner or Group Healing Technique

Purpose:

To enable you to spiritually share a physical experience with another person or a group of people, and to allow the synergy between all to aid in healing you or someone you love.

Application:

Practice this technique from time to time, as you wish, but not in place of your regular routine. You don't want to rely on anyone else to put you in contact with the Universal Energy.

If in a group, sit in a circle, so you can hold hands comfortably. If there are just two, face your partner. Place your right hand, palm down, over the next person's left hand, palm up, and continue until all hands are joined in this manner. Make sure that your hands rest comfortably on a leg, or something between you and the person next to you.

Procedure:

All close their eyes and center themselves. Once this is done, all should imagine energy, in the form of a blue-white light, coming in from their crown chakras and moving into their right hands and then the next person's left hand. Each person should feel the energy they receive from their partner's right hand and from the Universe. Each person imagines this energy as increasing and swirling through their body, the other bodies in the room, then expanding throughout the entire room. Then everyone imagines that the energy surrounds the room, then the building, and then the entire world. Keep this feeling going for a while, imagining the energy center is in the middle of the circle or between the partners.

Now each person projects anyone they want to help become happier or healthier into this energy center. You can even imagine your own body immersing itself in this beautiful elixir of energy. Imagine changing the color of the energy within this field from white and blue to pink, then to green, then back to white and blue. See whoever you project becoming healed. Imagine her face and smile. See and hear her dancing and singing. You are receiving this energy as well as the person you project, and both of you will feel it and become happier and healthier, if that is best for all.

When finished, count yourself out, one to five and open your eyes. Don't allow your hands to slip away from the others. If others have not finished, let them do so on their own. When everyone opens their eyes, release your hands and discuss and share the experience.

How it works:

By using a group or another person, you are within their auras, which helps energize each participant. Imagining energy as swirling is easier than if it is imagined as still. Changing the color brings different forms of energy (*i.e.*, healing, Love, awareness) into the projection. By putting people you want to help in the center, they'll receive what you are sending because it will be from Love. You'll be doing your part to make them happier and healthier. In turn, you'll be making the world a more loving place.

Additional comments:

It may be helpful to have a non-participant direct the action, or tape it and play it back, so everyone does the same things and ends at the same time. If you wear glasses, make sure to remove them, so they don't fall off.

Technique #16

The Grounding Technique

Purpose:

To increase your energy level and gain a sense of balance by connecting yourself to the earth and sky.

Application:

Do this whenever you need an energy boost or desire to feel more connected and balanced.

Procedure:

Sit upright in a chair and do the Basic Centering Technique. Then imagine a cord wrapped around your waist and the other end moving through your chair, the floor, the earth's crust, and the many layers of earth all the way to the earth's core. Now imagine it wrapped around the core of the earth. Imagine a second cord wrapped around your waist and the other end going above your head, through the roof and clouds, out of the earth's atmosphere, into deep space, and wrapping itself around a distant star.

Imagine a golden light emanating from the core of the earth and coming up slowly into you. Imagine a beautiful silvery light from the distant star and moving down the cord into you, as well. Imagine both these lights blending and feel the energy of the earth and sky within you. Remain in this state for as long as you desire, always visualizing the energy as moving up, down, around, and within you. When finished, imagine the cords coming back toward you, bringing with them all the energy you can handle. As you do, repeat the affirmation, "I am receiving all the energy I desire." Then count yourself out one to five, telling yourself that at the count of five you'll feel powerful, healthy, and fully energized.

How it works:

When centered you are in touch with the Universal Energy all around you. During this technique you direct this energy into you and control it to help energize you. It will. By keeping your feet flat on the ground, small chakras located in the soles of your feet absorb energy from the earth. Energy from above is received through the crown chakra.

Additional comments:

This is a good exercise to do with someone else or a group. You may want to first tape the exercise or have someone else read it to coordinate everything.

Lesson X

Direct The Universe!

"God appears to you not in person but in action."
Mahatma Gandhi

Are you ready to accept the responsibility that goes with realizing the power you have within? This power allows you to create a shift in your conscious awareness. Your responsibility is to create a fully awakened, happier world for you and your brothers and sisters. Your development also furthers the massive conscious shift toward the worldwide awakening we now celebrate.

As we work together to develop our spiritual awareness, we hasten the eventuality of our evolutionary journeys where we reunite with ultimate Love in another dimension. In this other dimension, we'll enjoy a new existence living only Love with all without needing comparisons to enjoy it.

We'll enjoy this wonderful dimension of Love until we decide, once again, to create what Love is not in another illusory world. We'll do this again and again so we can eternally know Love, living the perfect process of re-discovery.

Throughout this book, much information is offered to open your mind to the possibility that you're a perfect creation living and co-creating as part of the perfect process of the Universe. Developing your natural skills by practicing the sixteen centering techniques in this book lets you consciously co-create with Love. You'll realize your potential and discover how wonderful life can be.

By mastering these techniques, you'll receive answers directly from the Universal Intelligence. And you'll know they're right for you because they provide a feeling of Love and peace. You'll also be able to program for, and realize, anything you truly desire and receive any guidance sought. By centering yourself, you'll "direct the Universe" to work with and for you.

Each has his or her own unique way of receiving information and applying the power of the Universe. You can find out, through *results*, which techniques work best for you. After many successes, you'll no longer question your power. You'll only enjoy using this power to benefit humanity.

Remember what's important: that you are happy, healthy, wise, and wealthy, and consciously living and loving a purposeful life. Live the information in this book and you'll be on your way.

The techniques I've described are not the only methods for connecting with your Spiritual Self. But they do comprise a rounded program you can use for the rest of your life. If you use another method that works for you, continue using it, by all means. Positive results are what you desire. How you get them is unimportant.

"Whatever works for you..."

I remember a high school music class where a teacher whom I'll call Mr. J gave us many techniques to apply music theory. With Mr. J's help, I taught myself something I'll always remember. I share it so you don't get too caught up in the rituals of any program. Understand the purpose of a spiritual program is to put you in touch with God with loving results.

Whenever Mr. J offered a technique, I devised an alternative I thought was easier. Mr. J always invited me to explain my ideas to the class, offering them a choice. Some of the class preferred my methods, though Mr. J never seemed able to understand them. Time and time again, after getting frustrated by his inability to grasp my sometimes extravagant techniques, he'd give up and lovingly say, "Well, if it works for you, fine."

Whatever you've read here, you always have a choice what to believe and how to become fully awakened to your Spiritual Self. The glorious pleasures of this life await. You can be happier if you *do* realize you're a spiritual being and consciously live your soul's purpose on this planet. Any techniques or methods you employ to that end are fine, whether it's the program offered here or a different approach from another source, such as religion, prayer, or revelation from a life-changing experience. They are all ladders leading to the same place. Whatever works for you is fine.

Practice remembers perfect!

Developing your new skills takes practice, just like all skills. As you continue to practice these techniques, you're more able to recognize the types of feelings you get. Once you are familiar with your feelings in a centered state, Love will guide you, and you'll remember to trust those feelings. Your feelings will also become more clear and available to you as you practice and progress. By practicing you'll see the amazing results of trusting your Higher Self — your "intuition." You also become able to center yourself more quickly and easily. Each time you practice, your skill level increases. Centering has a cumulative affect. If you practice only once, then not again until a full year later, the second practice will still be more effective than the first.

Because it takes time to adjust to a new level of awareness, be patient. Make these techniques a part of your life and you'll reap the benefits forever. One of the best ways to accomplish this is to practice them daily as part of your routine. Practice the Basic Centering Technique, and then any other technique, at least twice a day, preferably right after you awaken and just before you sleep. A session after lunch is also a good time. But any time is better than no time.

Create a ritual. When you awaken, practice before getting out of bed. If you don't have the time to do a full fifteen minutes, simply take three deep diaphragmatic breaths or do whatever you can do. It's most important to do *something* and keep the routine going. You'll find that by making "sessions" a part of your everyday life, you benefit much more than if you have one only when you have "enough" time.

Feel free to add any practice aids you may desire, including scented candles, music, ocean sounds, etc. However, I suggest you eventually learn to do the techniques on your own to help develop your confidence in them and in yourself.

Some people find that by bringing more of the body into play with disciplines like yoga and tai chi, they can more easily integrate these techniques with the mind.[1] Try whatever you want, and keep what you like.

Make a conscious decision to be a more spiritually loving being in this existence. No one can do it for you. If you adopt the techniques, lessons, and applications from this book, you'll choose to be who you really are, doing what you really desire to do. This will benefit you and your loved ones, all of humanity, and the Universal Spirit.

Affirmations

Affirmations are powerful tools you can use to program yourself, reinforce previous programming, strengthen the immune system, and erase limiting belief systems. The lessons list many specific affirmations, and you can add these or others you create to any technique once you are centered. Simply repeat what you desire in a positive and accepting way, as if it were happening or had already happened. For example, you might say, "I feel great about my weight and am the healthiest size for me." In this case, it doesn't matter if you're telling the "truth," because you're programming (possibly in conjunction with the Theatre Technique) what you desire and reinforcing the new image in your mind. Don't say, "I want to be thinner," since you'd be telling the Universe you aren't thin and *that* will be the print-out you'll receive (Lesson VI). Believe, instead, that what you ask for has already occurred, and be thankful for your ability to achieve it.

Another use for affirmations besides adding them to your practice of the techniques for reinforcement, are as objects of focus. Center yourself and simply repeat one or more of these (or any others you choose) for an entire session: "I am surrounded by the Love of the Universe." "I am at peace with myself and with all other beings." Or, "All peace and Love begins within me."

If you repeat affirmations often enough, they sink into your unconscious mind and help print out what you're programming. Say, "I am a non-smoker" enough times, and your body starts to create this as a reality. If you've already programmed to quit smoking with the Theatre Technique, adding the affirmation, "I am a non-smoker" reminds the Universe and your body that this is your new reality. Believe that it will

---

[1] I find that most people seem to get better results without physical movement.

occur, accept that it has already occurred, and it will be created in the physical dimension if and when it is most beneficial for all involved.

Getting information

Lesson III told you how to know if information you receive is right for you and from the Universal Intelligence. There are many ways to receive this information. We've discussed getting information from your spirit guide through dreams or intuition. You may also get a clear message "out of nowhere," that you can see or hear. Or you may ask for a sign to know if something is beneficial for you, and then find that exact sign.

"When the student is ready, the teacher will appear." We are all-knowing beings. Signs and answers are always available to us, because our Higher Power is always with us. We need only allow ourselves to see them. We do so when we are acutely aware of what's around us, when we are "in-the-moment" spiritually.

Centering benefits

Centering provides many beneficial physiological and emotional "side effects." Although these benefits are desirable, remember the purpose of mastering your centering ability is to develop awareness of your Spiritual Self. All these techniques deepen your connection to the Almighty, helping you re-discover your true nature.

Some of the techniques in the book are modifications of methods developed centuries ago, while others are "new." All are designed to help you heal yourself and others. By applying them you direct the Universe to make your life and the world a happier and more loving place.

Both passive and active centering (also called "directed prayer") were used for the examples below. Find out what gets the best results for you. Once you do, stick with it. The first two examples are of physical and spiritual healing. They're not extraordinary examples but they're indicative of what can be accomplished when people are centered and can direct the Universal Energy.

Group "therapy"

Occasionally, I use the services of a healing group. People trained to use healing techniques agree to apply their skills at a certain specified time for several consecutive days to help someone overcome an unwanted condition.

A former seminar student called to say she'd been in a terrible car accident several months earlier and wasn't healing the way she'd hoped. She was in extreme pain, unable to work or sleep well, and afraid of getting addicted to pain medication.

I arranged a healing group and described her situation. That night, at exactly 10 p.m., we each centered ourselves and created an image of her as healed. Some took a passive approach by focusing on only the final image. Others were more actively involved by mentally "repairing" her injuries and sending energy to her.[2]

The next day she called to say she'd slept through the night for the first time since the accident. She also said she felt better. After a few days, she called again to inform me that she'd removed a cast, stopped taking the pain killers, and felt almost one hundred percent better. She was back to work a few days later.

You may ask, "Could it have been her taking the action to call and ask for help that caused her to improve?" Possibly, but it really doesn't matter how it works, just that it does! When we're centered we're all connected to each other and to the Universal Spirit. In this state of unity, there's actually only one Spiritual Energy at work.

Channeling away suffering

A seminar graduate suffering from cancer, told me he'd almost lost hope and wondered if there was anything that could be done. A few days later I centered myself and began sending energy in the form of a blue-white light, using the Channeling Technique described in Lesson VI. The next day he called and asked if I had done anything the night before. When I said yes, he asked when I'd done it. When I replied, "exactly 10:03 p.m.," he said, "I don't believe this! Right after ten I felt a sudden surge of energy rush through me. I felt as if someone else was there with me, helping me. I almost cried."

He called four days later and told me he was full of hope and felt peaceful for the first time in a long while. He knew he would be able to handle whatever happened and worried no longer.

A few weeks later, he called again to let me know that he'd received

---

[2] Either way, the final image should be of the desired result.

a good report from his doctor, and that he was happy. I didn't follow up to see if his cancer was gone completely, because the most important thing was that he was happy and not suffering.

Do your best to bring all of God's creations back to good health and remember everything that happens has purpose. It was up to my friend's mind to decide whether living or dying would best serve his purpose at the time. Our job is to allow that decision to be made through the other person's conscious control, by removing his fear and restoring his ability to see and pursue his purpose.

More results

Similar stories of physical, emotional and/or spiritual healing inspires us and helps us to see how powerful we truly are. These types of results may be obvious, but there are many other benefits to centering. Many forms of energy, including information, can be retrieved just by being in this powerful state of mind and awareness. You may be surprised at the types of information you can get and use as you continue to develop your spiritual awareness.

Here are a few examples that show how versatile these techniques, and you, really are.

The nationals trip

The annual National Softball Championship is an event I always looked forward to. At the time of the following incident, my wife was pregnant. The day before my nationals trip, she went to the doctor for a checkup. After tests, a nurse told her she might be dehydrated and might have to be hospitalized. The nurse took some additional tests, saying she'd have the results no earlier than 3:00 p.m. the next day. My flight was scheduled for 1:00 p.m., and I didn't know what to do. I couldn't leave if something was wrong, and there seemed no way to know before my flight.

I centered myself and quieted my mind using the Passive Centering Technique from Lesson VII. Instantly, I received a message, "The doctor knows the answer." It was just a thought that popped into my mind. It didn't make sense because the nurse assured my wife there was no possible way we would know before 3:00 p.m. the next day. However, I knew the answer was correct because I'd developed my skills enough to know I could depend on this type of message or feeling. I told my wife the answer I received, and she asked me to double check it. I repeated the process and was again given a clear message, "The doctor knows the answer." I assured her not to worry; we would call the doctor first thing in the morning and he'd have the answer.

The next morning we called the doctor, who told us the tests showed she was not dehydrated. After breathing a huge sigh of relief, my wife asked why the nurse told her what she did. The doctor said the nurse must have gotten confused. It turned out it was an insignificant test whose results would take until 3:00 p.m. to learn. Had I not asked while centered, or doubted my abilities, we'd never have thought to call the doctor.

Where there's smoke...

Someone in one of my seminars told me he once smelled smoke while centered. At the time, he was a thousand miles from home on vacation. He said it was so strong that he quickly got up and looked around, but nothing was burning. Soon after, he got a call that his house had burned down.

The important thing about this experience is that he had locked in an inner feeling and now had an opportunity to use the Success Tuning Technique from Lesson II. The next time he "psychically" smelled smoke, or had a similar feeling,[3] he'd know to take action since he'd be tuning into the feeling of "knowing," as he had in the original experience. He could now trust this same feeling to guide him in his current situation.

Inspection time

My wife and I have many talents between us. Unfortunately, taking care of our cars is not among them. This includes a lack of motivation to get them inspected on time as required by the law. We were more than an entire year late on one of our vehicles. This car was about two years old. We knew it was in good operating condition, and neither of us cared that it was overdue for inspection. To embarrass myself further, I must admit that we drove past an inspection station nearly every day!

It was amazing we never got pulled over. What could we have said?

---

[3] You may find that one of your "extra" senses seems to work better than the others. This is natural, and you should continue to look to receive information primarily with that sense.

"Uh, we didn't realize it was time for that?" I guess we were hoping that this excuse would prompt the officer who stopped us to let us go for giving him the best laugh he'd had in years.

One evening, on our way to dinner, I felt an urge to pull into the inspection station. When I told my wife, she asked what prompted the feeling. I told her I was thinking about something else when the feeling just came to me.[4] I told her I recognized this feeling and was sure we had to pull into the station, which finally ended our personal record of delinquency. She agreed. As we were getting the car inspected, I wondered why my intuition told me it was so important to do it right then. I was soon to find out.

After pulling out of the inspection station and turning the corner, we saw police stopping cars and checking their inspection stickers. Many cars with overdue stickers were pulled over. We politely smiled at the officers as we drove by. Our dinner that night was excellent.

The old man knows

The following is an example of getting information from a lucid dream. I'd been wondering what my Higher Self would say about homosexuality. Personally, I didn't have much of an opinion on the subject. But after listening to someone I respected tell a group that homosexuality was not the way of God, I decided to find out for myself. I programmed to have a lucid dream using the Lucid Dreaming Technique (Lesson IV). That night in a dream, I became lucid, that is, aware I was dreaming. I walked over to an old man[5] and asked him the true nature of homosexuality. Without hesitation he answered, "There's no such thing." I awoke thinking about this confusing answer and decided to center myself to determine what it meant. I understood the answer as this: there's no such thing as homosexuality from a spiritual sense. It's just a part of the physical world, an illusion like everything else in the physical dimension. There is no right or wrong in the spiritual world, no "male" and "female," and there is no true separation from one another. I wasn't expecting such an answer, but after thinking about it, it was the only possible answer that could have come from the Universe.

---

[4] I was using my intuition, which is sometimes received from my spirit guide described on page 188.

[5] Everyone in your dreams represents a connection to your Higher Self. Ask anyone questions and the answers will be from the Universal Intelligence.

My collection agency

During my softball years, I was paid to play for certain teams. On one occasion, after I quit a particular team, the owner didn't pay what he owed me. I encountered him again and again, and he always seemed to have an endless supply of excuses for why he couldn't pay. This went on for years. I knew he had the money and that I deserved what we'd agreed to.

In a centered state I programmed that every time he took a drink, he'd think of paying me. I used the Theatre Technique (Lesson V) and imagined seeing him in his home, taking a drink and feeling he must pay me. I did this for a week. When I saw him at a tournament that weekend, he nearly knocked someone over running to give me a check. His unconscious mind told him if he ever wanted to drink peacefully again, he'd have to give me what he owed.

An important note: If you operate at this dimension of mind, you can't make something happen that will hurt another, since it wouldn't be the loving thing to do. If you think about hurting another person, you'll pull yourself out of a centered state and will no longer be connected to the Universe. This doesn't mean that something "bad" won't happen; things sometimes happen from the cause-and-effect of our free will. But it won't happen with the help of the Universe.

In the above example, it was beneficial for the owner to pay me, so I did us both a favor.

Remarkable "dis" ability

Dreams are a link between your Higher Self and the physical world. If you pay attention to them, you'll receive timely information meant for you. Not all dreams have a spiritual theme. Some are just the workings of the mind from your occurrences of the past day. Some, however, are highly spiritual and contain true wisdom from God. To pay attention to your dreams and get information from them, first practice the Dream Log Technique described in Lesson IV. Then center yourself to decipher the dream's meaning.

In this dream, I entered a gymnasium or social club for the first time. Hundreds of people of all ages and races were there, all very relaxed and friendly toward one another, almost as if they were one family. Each person had a membership card and was supposed to sign in at the front desk. Even though I had a new membership card in my hand, I went past the desk without signing in to see if I could sneak by. No one stopped me. It seemed they didn't mind if I didn't sign in.

Moving past the desk, I noticed a movie theater set-up with no seats. I was standing near the balcony, which had about a forty-foot drop to the ground. There were no rails, and I wondered why people weren't worried about falling off. The only apparent way down was a staircase left of the balcony that reached to the main floor. People were walking up and down the stairs. Others were hanging around at the bottom.

As I watched the scene, I noticed a teenage boy in a wheelchair moving quite fast towards the balcony. I wondered why no one tried to stop him. I remember feeling sorry for him; there seemed no way for him to get down to the bottom. As he approached the ledge, he sped up and flew off the balcony! I was sure he'd hurt himself. But right before he hit the ground, he turned his wheelchair, by steering it in mid-air, and landed on the bottom step, face-up and smiling. No one but me was amazed at this. Actually, no one but me paid any attention at all to what he was doing. During the rest of the dream, the boy in the wheelchair showed up two more times. Each time he did something amazing. Again, each time, no one but me noticed. I was truly inspired.

Before I tell you what this dream meant to me, I remind you that if I hadn't paid attention to it or meditated on it afterwards (using the Dream Log Technique from page 105), it may have passed my conscious awareness without notice. We always have a choice to recognize and listen to our signs and messages.

This dream occurred while writing this book, and it's one example of the ways information came to me for it. While centered after the dream, I realized its message.

The club was a group of spiritually awakened people. They seemed like one big family because they realized they *were* all one family. I admired this group I'd apparently joined, because I had a membership card in my hand. As I went past the desk without signing in, I was testing the rules for being part of their spiritual community. They didn't care if I signed in or not, since there are no "rules" to be enforced in the spiritual world.

Of course, the most significant part of the dream was the boy in the wheelchair. He was able to do things that couldn't be explained by physical laws. His abilities went beyond anything I seemed to be able to do.

His purpose in the dream was to show me that I should not underestimate his power. He was also a member of the club and a spiritually awakened being. The others didn't notice him because they didn't see anything he was or did as unusual. He was their equal. Only I, in my naiveté, assumed he was someone to be concerned about. He was truly happy and having fun.

This dream told me this boy's soul had chosen this particular form to inspire and remind people that everyone is part of the perfection created by the Universe. It was obvious that I was the one in the dream with the disability. I was the one who needed inspiration and reminding that he was not all he appeared. This is one way I discovered that disabled people are inspirational souls who are here to lead others in their spiritual growth, and that everything was indeed part of the perfect process.

Now one might argue that this is what I wanted to believe and my unconscious mind created the dream's outcome to confirm what I wanted to happen. But, remember, everyone else in the dream saw him as normal. It was only I who saw him with a problem, which I must admit reflected my own stereotyped beliefs. It was only for my benefit that he turned and smiled, seeming to proclaim to me, "God is within me too. I am a perfect creation."

Lesson X summary:

There'll come a time when all humankind realizes that we are the creators of our world. When this occurs, we'll live happier, healthier, wiser, and wealthier lives. You can start now. You have the skills, the insight, and the ability to know the truth regarding the power of Love.

It is now time for you to direct the Universe! It is your time. Seize it!

Those who shine a light on others live in their shadow.

Never believe you are less wonderful than anyone else.

You have all the Love and light in the Universe within you.

Relax and feel the truth:

You are a perfect creation!

Amen.

Relax, You're Already Perfect

Index

Index

B

Balance 191, 192
Basic Centering Technique 26, 35, 39,
    41–43, 52, 54, 67, 166, 180, 183,
    193, 215, 219
Beethoven 154, 201
Belief systems 62, 63, 90–92, 146, 187,
    196, 202
    as an illusion 90
Berebi, Rabbi Eleazar HaKappar 138
Beta 28
Bible 22, 37, 46, 56, 60, 65, 134, 150,
    165, 171, 199
    interpretation of 37
Biofeedback 14
Birth choice 170, 205
Blasphemy 34, 61
Body 92–93, 102
Borysenko, Joan 148
Brain waves 27, 28, 102
Brow chakra 157
Buddha 32, 36
Buddhism 122, 151
Bukkyo Dendo Kyokai 151
Bulimia 24
Business 136, 152–155
    afirmations for 153
    prosperity 153
    using intuition for 155

C

Calling 14, 53, 63
Cancer 149, 222, 223
Capitalism 154
Casals, Pablo 201
Cause-and-effect 58, 144, 145, 147, 226
Cayce, Edgar 138
Centering 16, 18, 29, 38, 45, 52–54, 57,
    61, 63, 64, 67–69, 110, 140, 141,
    144, 155, 205, 218, 219, 221, 223
    benefits 221
Chakras 107, 143, 157–159, 161, 162,
    209, 216
    Balancing Technique 143, 157–159,
    161
    brow 157
    crown 157, 175, 182, 213, 216
    heart 157, 209

root 157
    solar plexus 157
    spleen 157
    throat 107, 157
Challenge 51, 189, 200
Chance 97–98
Change 92, 196, 197, 202, 210
Channeling Technique 161–162, 182,
    222
Children
    and discipline 204
    and education 206
    and meditation 206
    and religion 206
    and respect 202
    as intuitives 206
    as possesions 202
    developmental process of 204
    emotional development of 207
    raising perfect 206
    spiritual development of 207
    sports and hobbies 207
Choices 51–54, 57, 64
    making 52
Christianity 122
Church 34
Clergy 63
Coincidences 117, 136, 208
Communication 200, 205
    at the spiritual level 197
Competition 133, 207
Conflict 189, 196, 201, 206
Conners, Jimmy 142
Consequences 144
Constantine, Roman Emperor 123
Controversy 51
Creation
    process of 136, 146, 172
Creativity 191
Crimes and Misdemeanors 23
Crown chakra 157, 175, 182, 213, 216

D

Day, Dorothy 50
Death 60, 96, 163–165, 167
    fear of 60, 163
    purpose of 163
Deep Relax Technique 87–88, 175
Delta 28

232

Index

Index

Index

Order Form

Fax Orders: 1-732-792-0902

Telephone Orders: 1-888-962-7171 (Toll Free)
Please have your Discover, Visa, or MasterCard ready.

On-line: http://www.PerfectCreation.com

Mail Orders:
Ebb/Flow Publishing
22 Fallswood Lane
Manalapan, NJ 07726

Please send me _____ copies at $21.95 each of
Relax, You're already Perfect., ISBN 0-9673420-3-1
New Jersey residents, please add 6% sales tax.
Contact the publisher for quantity discounts.

Name: _____

Address: _____

City:_____ St:_____ Zip: _____

Telephone: (_____) _____

☐ Please send information about seminars, audio tapes, and other products.

Shipping:
$4.00 for the first book and $3.00 for each additional book.

Payment:
☐ Check Enclosed or
☐ Credit card: ☐ Visa ☐ MasterCard ☐ Discover

Name on Card: _____

Credit Card No: _____

Expiration Date: _____/_____